DAVE'S NOT HERE

*The Story of a man who had
to die to learn how to live*

DAVE'S NOT HERE

*The Story of a man who had
to die to learn how to live*

DAVE FRIDLUND

XULON PRESS

Xulon Press
2301 Lucien Way #415
Maitland, FL 32751
407.339.4217
www.xulonpress.com

ISBN-13: 978-1-5456-7350-8

To Robynn.

You have saved my life on more than one occasion.
I love you!

Acknowledgments:

*T*hanks *to my family and friends who have always had my back, especially when the odds were stacked against me.You bombarded heaven with your prayers, relentlessly sought God on my behalf, and made it possible for me to be here to tell my story. Your reward in Heaven will be greater than all the gratitude I could ever offer in this book.*

SPECIAL THANKS:

To Brad, Angie, and the entire Williams family for being such a support and blessing to my family over the years; and to Randy and Gina Conrad for constantly encouraging me to write this book from the first page to the last.

To Winston Sanders, for your twenty-five plus years of friendship and for offering to edit this book. Your input is invaluable and I hope this is the first of many projects we collaborate on.

To my children–Alison, Jessica, Jacob, Kenneth, and Kyle.
I continue to be in awe of your humility and character. Thank you for your unconditional love and support, and for listening to all of my many stories. You

are wise beyond your years. In this life, you are my greatest reward.

To Rex and Shelly Pierson, and Pastor Tray Jenkins, who jumped into action and were the first on the scene to pray for me at Sunrise Hospital.

What you accomplished in the spiritual as well as the natural realms did not go unnoticed.

To all the Pastors who were influential throughout this story:

Pastor Rusty George–Real Life Church in Valencia, California
Pastor Shane Philip–The Crossing in Las Vegas, Nevada
Pastor Tray Jenkins–The Crossing in Las Vegas, Nevada
Pastor John Koczman–Bethlehem SCV in Canyon Country, CA.

Thank you for being shining examples of what true followers of Christ look like.

Finally, to the hundreds of people who prayed for me during the first 48 hours. I stand as a living testimony that God heard your every word.

Endorsements:

"This is an amazing yet true, real life story of hope, healing and a man's journey through death to find life!"

Rusty George
Lead Pastor, Real Life Church, Valencia, CA.

"Very refreshing and authentic. Dave's style is nothing less than sincere and draws me in to want to hear more. I pray and hope all of us have moments of awakening and revival".

John Koczman
Senior Pastor, Bethlehem SCV, Canyon Country, CA.

"It wasn't an accident that our paths crossed. Dave's pastor, my closest ministry friend of 40 years, texted me on a Sunday morning to see if one of our pastors could go see Dave in the hospital in Las Vegas. He had just had a major stroke and they didn't know if he was going to make it. I immediately asked Tray Jenkins, one of our pastors, to step in to be there for the family. God uses each of us for such a time as this".

"You are going to be blessed by Dave's story and his journey with God".

Shane Philip
Senior Pastor, The Crossing, Las Vegas, NV.

"God is still in the business of performing miracles, not just for those who personally experience them, but also for those who witness them.

This story is not about Dave, it's about the living God supernaturally revealing Himself to Dave and to our world..I was there, and I'm a witness."

Tray Jenkins
Associate Pastor, The Crossing, Las Vegas, NV

"Daves real life encounter is a testimony of how Jesus drew him closer than he could ever have imagined through a time of simultaneous trials and blessings.

But more than that, his story is intended for us all, and encompasses more than just the experiences them-selves. It speaks of the importance of ongoing com-munion, communication, prayer, spiritual warfare, and how God wants to use His sons and daughters to trans-form the world around us for His Kingdom.

It's about the need for revival, and how each one of us can escalate and transcend our individual experiences and ultimately come together to set the world on fire for His Glory."

Winston Sanders
Founder and President, National Prayer Rallies and-
Prayer on the Air Radio ministries

About The Author:

*D*ave Fridlund is a follower of Jesus Christ, husband to Robynn,
Step-Father and Father-in-Law to Ali and Ryan, Father to Jessie, Jake, Kenny and Kyle, and proud Grandpa to little Annabella, Clark,... and counting!

Last but not least, daddy to a sixteen and a half-year-old puppy named Pepper, with whom I will be running through the hills of Heaven one day...unleashed!

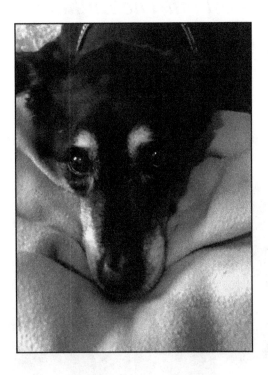

What's my story?

I'm that guy! The one who spent most of his life lying, cheating and posing as a Christian. I was an impostor. A phony. I thought I knew Jesus. I heard all the sermons. I even owned a Bible with my name engraved on the cover.

As I said, I was an impostor, and I fooled a lot of people...just not Him!

My story is simple. It's about my desperate need to die to myself before I could learn how to live for Jesus.

This book is a collection of true accounts chronicling what I shared with family and friends through a series of social media posts, illustrating how Jesus pulled me out of my own self inflicted darkness and into His brilliant light.

So follow along and witness the profound, miraculous events that shaped my life and transformed me from a part-time churchgoer to a full-time follower of Christ.

The following accounts chronicle the three and a half year period that changed my life and those around me... forever.

POST #1

June 27, 2015

Dear family and friends,

I'm finally home and recovering slowly from heart surgery. Many amazing things happened to me over the last three weeks, and I thought it would be good therapy to write down a detailed account while the memories are still fresh in my mind.

If you will all humor me, I'd like to start at the very beginning and share those memories and events as they happened.

POST #2

Just another Friday?

My story begins on a Friday Morning, June 5th, 2015.

I had just woken up from a decent sleep. "A lot going on today!" said my wife. She has every Friday off, and usually has a laundry list of things that need to get done. My daughter was in town with her boyfriend, who had just asked for her hand in marriage.

1

Still, in my pajamas, I proceeded to the bathroom to brush my teeth. On the way, I pulled a muscle under my right shoulder blade. My wife was still laying in bed as I paced the bedroom floor trying to relax the muscle. The pain moved to my left shoulder blade as I continue pacing. My wife said to me, "Why don't you lie on the bed and I'll massage it out for you?" The second she said that, I started feeling heartburn. I immediately asked Robynn, "What did I eat last night?"

As the heartburn increased, so did my wife's concern. She pulled out her iPad and began diagnosing my symptoms. Slowly, the heartburn subsided, only to be replaced by a metallic taste in my mouth. The taste continued as I thought to myself, *"I'm gonna be sick right now."*

I made my way to the bathroom just a few feet away, bent my head down toward the toilet bowl and prepared to hurl. Nothing came out! As fast as the symptoms appeared, they went away! *"That was weird!"* I thought. "Well, I feel fine now," I told my wife, as I proceeded to get on with my day. "Not so fast," she said, as she began to deliver her diagnosis.

TO BE CONTINUED…

POST #3

"I think you just had a little heart attack," my wife said. "Get ready, I'm taking you to the hospital," she continued. Usually, I'd be quick to dismiss something like that, but that day was different. So, we threw on some clothes and drove to our local Emergency Room.

Now you have to understand, as we traveled to the hospital, I started to feel fine. The longer we drove, the more I thought that going to the ER was overkill, but Robynn was driving with purpose and if I knew what was good for me, I figured I better just sit there, shut up and go along with it. After all, they were just going to check me out and send me back home anyway! When we arrived and were checking in, I overheard my wife telling the receptionist, "It's a possible heart attack," and instantly the wheelchair came flying around the corner! From there, I was rushed to a private room and slapped onto a gurney as my shirt came off and the heart monitoring devices came on! *"Wow,"* I thought, *"this is the real deal!"*

After a blood test and an X-ray, the doctor came back and said, "Well, the good news is, you didn't have a heart attack," looking at me with a smile.

"Cool," I was thinking. *"Let's get outta here and go to the mall."*

"There's something I'm concerned about!" he said (this time WITHOUT a smile).

TO BE CONTINUED...

3

POST #4

"There's something I'm concerned about!" said the Doctor. "It looks like you have Atrial Fibrillation" (that's when your heart literally beats to its own drummer). *"Sounds like me,"* I thought. "We'd like to do some more tests," he said with a puzzled look on his face. I reluctantly agreed, as the doctor ordered a type of ultrasound called an Echocardiogram. Minutes later, he returned with the news that I had an aortic aneurysm. *"Okay, that's nice, but what does that mean?!"* I thought.

What it meant was that I had an abnormal bulge in my aorta, caused by a defective valve that I apparently was born with. Something that could end my life at any moment!

My aorta was five centimeters wide. The danger zone is five point five centimeters for an average heart! The doctor told us it could be as far out as a year, but it could also happen as soon as a month or even a day when my aorta would eventually rupture. He went on to say, "And even if you're lucky enough to be in a hospital when your aorta bursts, there's still a twenty percent chance you'll die instantly."

I guess no one will ever know.

The important thing, and one that I need to remind myself of daily, is that my life was saved that day! So, to both God and my wife, thank you!!!

After receiving the news, the doctor went on to tell me that he'd (obviously) feel more comfortable if I stayed overnight for a few more tests. I was thinking, *"You've got to be kidding me!" I just got hired on with a new company, and I have to get ready to travel any day now!"* Of course, nobody was listening. All I saw was that ugly gown coming my way and my wife telling me to strip down. Little did I know, that ugly gown would become my only wardrobe for the next three weeks!

All of a sudden, I found myself being wheeled off to a room with no view. There were two beds, and one was already occupied by a man who just had a heart attack. *"I can handle one night! They'll do some tests, give me a prescription and send me on my way,"* I thought to myself.

I had just gotten hired with a new company after spending the last six months in the interview process, and I wasn't going to blow it by calling in sick before I even started!

As resolved as I was to start my new career, any ideas of me leaving that hospital were quickly squashed when a new doctor entered my room and introduced himself as a heart surgeon. "You're going to need surgery ASAP!" he blurted out. *"Wow, that was blunt,"* I thought.

While he was sitting on the end of my bed sharing the news, two nurses were simultaneously sticking needles in my veins. *"Is this really happening?"* I thought to myself. *"Oh yeah, and at lightning speed."*

I was in complete shock, and I remember mumbling, "Oh crap!"
TO BE CONTINUED...

POST #5

"Oh crap!" was exactly what I said. Up until that point, I assumed we were talking about some possible operation way out in the future (which on its own was horrific enough) but this dude was actually talking about the next few days! *"Are you kidding me, I can't accept this,"* I thought frantically.

I even considered the possibility that the surgeon was having financial problems and needed my business. *"Maybe he was late on his Mercedes payment?"* That would explain why he was pushing this whole operation thing so hard! My mind was racing, my heart was pounding and my blood pressure was soaring. I literally felt like a caged animal! I couldn't move because I had tubes coming out of me, people were on every corner of my bed, and I was starting to hyperventilate. All I wanted to do was get up and leave, but the doctors and nurses wouldn't let me. What a horrible feeling! And on top of all that, my wife seemed to be going along with the whole thing!

An intense feeling of paranoia set in, along with denial, anger, and depression. It all hit at once. I was mentally and emotionally overwhelmed and going downhill fast! That wisecracking, jovial guy who never took anything serious had just been hit by a "freight train" called reality.

TO BE CONTINUED…

POST #6

The downward spiral of my emotions must have been very obvious to those around me, because one of the nurses appeared with a very large needle and told me "this will calm you down." Reluctantly, I let her stick me again and after a few more minutes of hyperventilating, I finally started to relax.

At one point, my wife went home to pick up a few things for me, since I wasn't going anywhere for awhile. Once calm, I asked the nurse if I could use the bathroom, so she helped me out of bed and showed me how to wheel my IV stand to the restroom in the far corner of the room. As I was passing the patient in the bed next to me, I noticed he was looking straight at me. I said, "Hi, how are you doing?" Well, if looks could kill, I'd definitely be on my way out. This guy stared me down as if I had just shot his dog. I thought to myself, "*Whatever.*"

It's not like my day could get any worse!

TO BE CONTINUED...

POST #7

I finished my business in the bathroom. As I opened the door to go back to my bed, I thought to myself, "*I'm not going to even look at this guy. He's obviously a jerk and could care less about what others are going through.*" So I just blew him off and went back to my side of the room.

Right about that time, Robynn returned with some of my belongings. One important item was my iPad. With my stress level up so high, she thought it would be nice for me to have access to some Christian music. *"Who knows, it might even help my roommate with his attitude problem."* I thought.

As I quietly laid in my bed listening to my music (trying not to tick anyone off) I heard the guy making a phone call. All I could hear him say was, "Honey, it's Dad." "I'm sorry, he didn't make it... he's gone. I tried everything but I couldn't save him...I couldn't."

He began crying uncontrollably while saying, "I'm sorry, I'm so sorry."

"I was holding him when he died...he died in Daddy's arms baby. Please come and get me," he said. "Please, I don't know what to do. I'm in a hospital and I'm going crazy. Please come and get me right now."

After he gave her the room number, he hung up. I could still hear him crying.

That's when I lost it! The tears poured out of me like a fountain, as I asked God to help this guy. That's when I realized how pathetic I was being. *"How could I have been so self-absorbed,"* I thought.

Later, I found out he was brought in that morning by ambulance after suffering a heart attack, due to stress.

That poor guy had a heart attack as a result of watching his own son die in his arms and I had the gall to gripe about my problems! My heart broke for that man...That father.

TO BE CONTINUED…

POST #8

Crack in the armor

I laid in that hospital bed, crying like a baby. I don't think I had ever cried like that before. Especially for some guy I didn't even know or care about. But, at that moment in time, I cared like he was my brother. I couldn't control the pain that was inside my heart for that man. I just think that for a short while God wanted me to take on the burden of some of his pain. I tried to stop myself from crying, but it hurt too much.

I couldn't control my emotions.

Doctors were coming in and out of the room and still assuming I was upset over the news of my operation. I actually had to explain what was going on with me and asked them for some time to compose myself. By then, the man's daughters arrived. Two girls about fifteen and twenty. They walked right past my bed, looked right through me with that same stone face the father had displayed earlier. When they saw their dad, they just broke. They were all sobbing, and I was tearing up just listening to them. I heard the father say, "Just get me out of here."

A few minutes later, he was dressed and ready for discharge. The doctor and nurse came in and told him to go home and take it easy. His daughters gathered his belongings and proceeded out of the room. I was wiping my eyes as he walked by. He didn't look at me. *"I have to say something,"* I thought to myself. I couldn't stand to see him go before letting him know he wasn't alone, so I just blurted out "excuse me!"

He stopped in his tracks and looked right at me with those same eyes. It was a look like, "You talking to me?" My words tumbled out, "I was listening to what was going on and I just wanted to say I'm so sorry for your loss." I think he noticed I was visibly upset, so he paused, took a breath and said, "Explain to me, what kind of person sells heroin to a twenty-two-year-old kid in Santa Clarita...Santa Clarita?" I looked at him and just kept saying, "I'm sorry, I'm so sorry."

He walked out, his two daughters followed. They, in turn, looked at me. The complete lack of hope in their eyes was heart-wrenching. I know now, God needed me to experience that. He needed me to see hopelessness up close. That experience helped me realize what Jesus must feel every day. His heart must ache nonstop for the world.

Jesus said to them all, "if anyone wishes to follow me, he must die to himself, take up his cross and follow me". (Luke 9:23)

I was left alone in that room, faced with the reality of a man who would never see his son again. Ever!

There would never be a way to fix that. It was final and I just couldn't comprehend it.

I saw stories like those on the news for years and it never affected me. In fact, I've never lacked for opinions on the subject, nor had I ever had a problem judging other people's situations from the comfort of my armchair. There's always been a clear separation between everyone else's heartaches and my own. I always thought I felt for others. I just can't remember ever feeling so emotionally invested in someone else's life like that. It was strange to me and hard to shake.

Throughout the rest of that day, doctors and nurses were coming in and out, and each time I had to explain why I was crying. Again, they all must have assumed that I was still distraught over the thought of open heart surgery, and because of that, the sedatives started coming out of the woodwork!

I sat in that bed thinking, *"My heart's broken and all they can offer me are more drugs?"*

TO BE CONTINUED...

POST #9

Bill the Newsman

Toward the end of that day, they decided to move me to another room.

This was an upgrade! It was a room that faced the sun, and I had my own window.

The downside? My new roommate was a screamer. His name was Bill, a former newsman who had a plethora of problems. He was old, senility was setting in, and his body was slowly shutting down. Because of that, he constantly screamed and shouted to the nursing staff, all day and all night.

"What a horrible roommate to be matched up with!" some might say.

Oddly enough, my heart went out to that man, and I was happy to be there.

TO BE CONTINUED...

POST #10

I was in my new room. I had Bill to the left of me. We were separated by a curtain, and, as I remember, he was asleep when they wheeled me in. Basically, he had no idea that he was sharing his room with another person. That in itself, became quite humorous. Whenever he became delirious, I took it upon myself to calm him down. When he screamed for a nurse, I would speak to him in a low, calm voice, saying, "Everything's going to be okay, Bill. Just have faith and believe in Jesus." All of a sudden he would stop yelling. I think he thought I was the voice of God. He never answered; ever. He just listened and calmed down. It was awesome!

When I arrived at that second room, I was still quite shaken about the father losing his son. I didn't want to just forget what happened to me in that first room, but at the same time, I also didn't want to carry that burden any longer. I remember asking God to take that feeling of sadness away from me and replace it with peace.

I couldn't recall the exact Scriptures at the time, but I remembered the Bible talked about the "peace that passes all understanding," and "His peace will guard your heart and mind as you live in Christ Jesus". I also knew the Apostle Paul wrote that in his letter to the Philippians, and I figured that since he had been shipwrecked, thrown into prison, beaten, stoned and eventually beheaded, he probably was a guy who had a pretty good idea of how to tap into the peace of God. So, I prayed for that same peace he was given. It didn't happen instantly, but I kept on asking.

I knew if I was going to get through this ordeal, I would need something outside of myself. I just remember that something broke inside of me, and I started asking God to forgive me for everything in my life that wasn't pleasing to Him. I had a laundry list of stuff I needed to make right with Him. From the obvious things, to the secret sins I didn't even want to admit I had. I don't remember ever in my life getting that serious with God. Something was definitely happening. The old Dave was slowly being erased.

By the end of the day, right before my wife came back, I was starting to feel happy. Genuinely happy... almost giddy! It was true peace. I asked for it, and He delivered. Big time!

I had trouble understanding how it was possible to feel so happy, considering everything that happened over the last few hours. All I knew was, I needed that feeling to last. It was better than any drug they could have given me. I was literally overflowing with peace and joy. God's Spirit hovered over my room that day. He showed up exactly when I needed Him, and that's the moment I felt gratitude.

TO BE CONTINUED...

POST #11

That first night in the hospital, Bill was very active. He started talking to himself about 3:00 AM. I can't actually say he was talking to himself, it sounded more like he was talking to several other people. "Let this meeting come to order," he said boldly. Bill was obviously transported back to a better time and place where he was clearly the "Man in charge." As far as I could tell, he was very unhappy about the way the network was performing and there were several heads on the "chopping block." He conducted his meeting for about half an hour before the nurses came in to turn him.

Bill couldn't move on his own, so the staff had to turn him from side to side about every hour or so. They didn't want him to get bed sores because that would add a whole new set of problems to what he was already contending with. I felt bad for Bill. He was just starting to get into his board meeting when reality reared its ugly head. I can only imagine what was going through his mind. Here's a guy who was obviously a very powerful man at one point in his life. He had a lot of respect and a lot of responsibility in the network news business. A huge portion of his identity for many years must have been his career. When that came to an end, I imagine, so did a large part of his life. Now he had a chance to relive that life through his dreams, only to be rudely interrupted by a nurse emptying his bedpan. How very sad.

As soon as Bill realized he was only having a dream, the screaming would start right back up again, the nurses would run right in and my cue to pray would begin! While he was awake, it took several nurses to keep him under control. They rationed his pain meds, so every couple of hours, like clockwork, he'd be begging for more. As you would expect, the 3:00 AM shift was tough on those poor nurses. They would periodically peak their heads through the curtain to see how I was doing. At one point, they even apologized to me on Bills behalf. One nurse called me a "Saint." All I knew was that God put me in that room for a reason, and if it was to wake up at three o'clock in the morning to pray for Bill, then that's what I would do. I had a sense of purpose in that room, with that particular man at that particular time in his life.

God gave me great peace to deal with the pain and uncertainty in my own life. I just prayed He would do the same for Bill.

TO BE CONTINUED...

POST #12

I spent the next several days at Henry Mayo Hospital. The days were packed with visitors, doctors and nurses scheduling tests, and of course, drawing blood from every available vein in my body. I didn't mind. The peace I was given days earlier still remained. Bill was constantly up and down. One day, he had visitors from the news station. There were "on-air" personalities and television executives coming and going all day and Bill seemed very lucid while they were around, but the minute they left, he would immediately become scatterbrained again, yelling at nurses and screaming for help. I didn't know how to help him. All I could do was pray harder.

One day, a pastor came to his room. He seemed to know Bill and kept telling him how everyone at his church had been praying for him. He sounded like a nice man. Come to find out, he was the Senior Pastor of a christian church that Bill's daughter attended.

Bill had gone there a few times over the years with his daughter. What made that so unusual was that Bill was Jewish. I figured this out when one of his friends asked him if he'd still been going to his temple, and he said he'd been going to church with his daughter, who had become Christian. His friend just said, "Oh, really, that's interesting." I don't think Bill was totally comfortable with it, but I know one thing for sure, he really needed Gods intervention...so I kept praying.

A couple of days later, Bill's daughter was talking to him and I heard her say, "Dad, I called your brother in New Jersey and he wants to fly out tomorrow and see you." Bill didn't sound pleased. "I don't want to see that guy," he said. His daughter pleaded with him, "Dad, you haven't talked to him in 25 years. It's time to bury the hatchet."

Reluctantly, he agreed to the visit. This told me a lot about his condition.

I knew then, Bill was dying. His body was slowly shutting down and his daughter knew it, and all she cared about was her dad finding peace, with everyone including God.

That same day, a nurse came in and said to me, "I have good news!" "We found a new room for you." "Now you don't have to listen to Bill all night and you can get some rest."

I was just as surprised as the nurses when I turned down the offer. One nurse asked me why and all I could say was, "I think Bill needs me here." I just remember the look on her face when she said, "You are a saint." I laughed and said, "Oh, if you only knew."

TO BE CONTINUED...

POST #13

Over the next few days, I continued to pray for Bill.

During that time, the resident surgeon would come to my room to discuss the timeline for my surgery. I was unsure as to the right decision to make, when it came to a mechanical valve versus a biological one. There were two ways to go—a cow or pig valve called Bovine or Porcine or a man-made appliance. If I chose a natural valve, then I only had a ten to fifteen-year expiration date before I had to upgrade the valve, through another operation. If I chose an appliance, it would last for a lifetime. The bad news...I would have to take blood thinners every single day, for the rest of my life.

The surgeon had a definite opinion as to the direction he preferred. He was pushing for a mechanical valve. I, on the other hand, wasn't ready to become "RoboDave" just yet. Also, the thought of being chained to blood thinners for the rest of my life didn't sit well with me. It just seemed so final. If there was a chance to be free from drugs one day (which were extremely hard on the body) I wanted to take it. My surgeon didn't seem to have that opinion and it really bugged me. I couldn't put my finger on it, but there was something I didn't like about that guy. Maybe I was just overreacting, but I told my wife that I wanted a second opinion. I felt like I was being pushed into something I wasn't comfortable with. At that point, I knew what was needed. I had to just step back and ask God to take over. So, that's what I did. And that's when the miracle happened!

Out of the blue, my wife received a call from her stepsister. She heard through the grapevine that I was in the hospital and took it upon herself to contact someone that would play a key part in what was to come.

Evidently, her Sister-in-law (who Robynn and I met briefly at her wedding) just happened to work for a top manufacturing company that supplies heart valves for the medical industry. In a matter of an hour, my wife was sending my echocardiogram to the top executives at this company for their medical opinions. Not only that, but the company's senior executive personally referred my case to one of the top heart surgeons in the world (who just happen to be a close friend of his) and asked him to rearrange his schedule at UCLA Medical Center to fit in my emergency surgery ASAP!

It was mind-boggling how quickly the pieces were falling into place, but I wasn't out of the woods just yet! There would be another major obstacle to overcome. Would our HMO allow me to transfer from our local hospital to one of the most elite medical centers in the world? In addition, would our insurance plan cover the added cost?

TO BE CONTINUED...

POST #14

Just a coincidence?

We were waiting patiently to hear back from Facey Medical Group about our proposed transfer to UCLA Medical Center, and if our HMO would even cover the expenses. It would be a lot of work for nothing if they said no. Not only did my Sister-in-law (Mindy) go out on a limb with her Sister-in-law (Mandy), but Mandy brought in the big guns by asking one of the executives at her company to personally help orchestrate my transfer, not to mention asking the Chief of Cardiac Surgery at UCLA to perform the procedure.

We were all going out on a very long limb and hoping it wouldn't snap. The amazing thing was that I felt no pressure or worry whatsoever, but rather total confidence that everything was taken care of in advance! I literally sat back and watched the whole scenario play out right before my eyes. It used to be very hard for me to completely give up control to anyone, especially Jesus. I knew the day had come to finally put my money where my mouth was and let God go about His business. Up to that point, He hadn't disappointed me and I was amazed at how easy it was to just let go.

Note: Several days later -
I was recovering in the ICU after my heart surgery. My surgeon, Dr. Richard Shemin, stopped by to check on my recovery progress and we start talking.

"How do you know so and so," he asked (referring to the executive at the valve manufacturing company).

I just laughed and said, "I don't." He looked puzzled. "Let's just say that was a miracle," I said. He looked at me, smiled and said, "Yes sir, that was!"

POST #15

Back at Henry Mayo Hospital, I continued to trust in the process. Everything looked like it was a "go" on the transfer. The only thing we were waiting on was the news of an available bed at UCLA. Then, I would be on my way.

Well, soon after that, we received the good news that a bed had recently opened up! We were just waiting on the logistics. That was day seven at Henry Mayo Hospital. I had most of my tests and even my angiogram at that hospital. They were very good to me, and I can't say enough about the staff and the doctors. Wonderful people!

As my time was running down, I continued to pray for Bill. I hadn't seen much improvement since I became his roommate, but he still needed my prayers.

After dinner that evening, one of the nurses came into my room to let me know a bed was available at UCLA and I would be heading over that night. It wasn't until 9:00 pm before an ambulance would arrive to transfer me. I was feeling calm, my blood pressure was normal and I was ready to go. After saying my goodbyes to the staff and one last prayer for Bill, I was on my way.

I arrived at UCLA Medical Center at 10:15 pm. The place was packed. Even the ambulance driver said he had never seen so many people. It was standing room only in the ER. Patients were lined up in the hallway, some were crying, some were sick and even bleeding as I passed right by them.

The EMT's wheeled me to an elevator. I headed directly to the seventh floor (oddly enough) where I had a private room waiting for me, overlooking Bruins Stadium and a 40" flat screen TV on the wall. A far cry from the "war zone" downstairs. *"This wasn't so bad,"* I thought. The nursing staff greeted me and made sure I was comfortable. By that time, it was pushing 11:00 pm. I just assumed that it would be a quiet, uneventful evening (like the ones at Henry Mayo) and I would get eight hours of blissful sleep before the doctors started their morning rounds.

Oh, how I couldn't have been more wrong!

TO BE CONTINUED...

POST #16

It's gonna hurt...a lot!

Just as I was anticipating a nice, relaxing night's sleep, I heard a knock on the door. It was a young female doctor who identified herself as one of Doctor

Shemin's team members. Doctor Shemin was the surgeon who would be performing my open heart surgery. The young doctor and an entourage of about four or five others swarmed me like a bunch of hungry crows around a garbage can. I thought to myself, *"Okay, five or ten minutes, they'll get bored and leave."* That wasn't the case. After assessing my vitals and a few concerned looks, I heard someone say, "We need to get him into ICU STAT"

"Wait," I thought, *"Isn't that Intensive Care?"* Just then, a nurse leaned in and said, "Mr. Fridlund, your blood pressure is dangerously high and we need to stabilize it quickly. Just try to relax." *"Just try to relax?...I was until you guys came in!"*

They didn't mess around. My bed (with me in it) was urgently transported down the hallway. It was like a scene out of ER...only I'm the expendable actor who dies and is never seen again!

We arrived in the ICU and a whole new set of doctors appeared. One was already dressed in scrubs and a mask, as though she was prepared for surgery. I jokingly said, "Looks like you're getting ready to operate! Isn't that a little dramatic?"

She looked at me with extreme concern on her face and just said, "Sir, I'm gonna need to open up a couple of arteries right now...so we can run a line to monitor your vitals."

I immediately replied, "Oh, okay. Your gonna put me under...right?" She shook her head and said, "No Sir, we don't have time." My voice shook as I asked, "Is it

23

gonna hurt?" Her response was, "I'm not gonna lie to you. It's gonna hurt A LOT!"

TO BE CONTINUED…

POST #17

Let the pain begin!

When a doctor begins a sentence like "I'm not gonna lie to you", you know you're in for a world of hurt! I already had multiple tubes coming out of me, but that was clearly not enough for these guys. I was definitely pampered at Henry Mayo Hospital. My biggest decision was what flavor pudding I would have for dessert, and my blood pressure was just fine. *"How is it, I've only been at UCLA for five minutes and I already have all these problems?"* I thought to myself.

I watched as the doctor laid out all of her very sharp instruments, while at the same time, strapping down my left arm. "Now, Mr. Fridlund is it?" "Correct," I answered, in a "not so jovial" voice. "You're going to feel some pressure on your left wrist," she said politely. I was thinking, *"After being brutally honest just two minutes ago, now you're gonna use that famous line, spoken by every dentist in America, right before they jam a three-inch needle through the roof of your mouth?!"*

"Not today lady." I thought to myself, until I realized I had no vote in the matter. I felt a little pressure alright! All I could say was, "A little pressure, huh? Oh,

24

man! You're killing me here!" "You're doing great, Mr. Fridlund," she commented.

Her definition of "doing great" and mine, seemed to be miles apart!

It's hard to describe the pain. When you get to a certain point, it becomes hard to tell exactly where it's coming from. I had an idea in my head of what was happening to my wrist, but I tried my best to block it out.

They needed to open my main artery, run a wire through the vain, which gives a more accurate reading of my blood pressure, and then, immediately suture the artery back up, so I don't bleed out and die! The latter, being the most important...of course!

Just as I was thinking to myself, "She should probably be finished by now," she said, "Okay, all I need to do is put about four sutures in this and we'll be done!" Then she said something that I'll never forget, "Why don't you count with me?" *Did she just ask me to count with her? What is this, a children's show?*" I thought. Guess what? I counted with her, and it didn't help. It still hurt like hell! After finally sewing and bandaging my wrist, she said, "Now Mr. Fridlund, I just need to make one more incision in your neck and we'll be all done!" "*AGAIN WITH THE ALL DONE!*" I screamed to myself! "*Huh? Are you being serious!*"

TO BE CONTINUED...

POST #18

That doctor just finished running a line through the artery in my wrist. *"Wow, that was fun!"* I thought. Now, all I have to do is let her slice open my neck and "We'll be all done!" she stated in a perky voice.

Before I could protest, the nurse on my right began covering up my entire head with a rubber sheet. The only opening in that sheet was a small square that was cut out and placed directly over the main artery in my neck. I immediately felt my breath against the rubber sheet. It steamed up quickly as I realized that there was no hole for my nose or mouth. I couldn't breathe! It was like the time I put a plastic bag over my head as a kid and then thought,

"Uh oh! This was a mistake!"

I politely let the doctor know that if she insisted on covering my head like that, I would probably suffocate to death long before she could slash my throat!

She said, "Don't worry Mr. Fridlund, it'll be over soon." "I can't keep this on, I'm gonna pass out!" I said forcefully. Her answer to me was, "Just relax."

Just then, all hell broke loose in my mind! All the peace I had coming into this hospital, managed to disappear with those same two words, "Just relax." I felt extremely agitated. All I wanted to do was get up, jump off that table and get out of there. For the first time in my adult life, I felt claustrophobic.

I realize now that I was having another panic attack! All I could think about at the time, was how I was suffocating to death, at the same time that doctor was cutting open my throat. It was horrible!

I asked the doctor if she could just give me one minute to collect myself. Then I asked the nurse to please hold the end of the plastic sheet up, so I could feel like there was fresh air coming in, and finally, I prayed and asked God to please give me the strength to get through this procedure. I remember praying to myself, *"Please help me, Jesus."*

The doctor asked me, "Are you ready now?" I said, "Uhh, sure."

The doctor and the entire nursing staff received a quick lesson on how to "pray without ceasing." I was literally talking out loud to Jesus while she was operating. I kept laughing and telling Him, "You've got to be kidding me, Lord," as the doctor cut deeper. There is a point people reach on their personal pain threshold, where it doesn't even hurt anymore. Where your mind has trouble identifying what pain is and where it's coming from. At least, that's what appeared to be happening to me. So, I laughed, joked with God, giggled and laughed some more (out loud and unfiltered) until it was all over.

God was there for me! He was in that room! Did He take away the pain? No, but I do know He was holding my hand! I also know that He gave me the strength to get through it.

I've seen that bumper sticker for years, "LET GO AND LET GOD".

Well, during that emergency surgery I was given no choice but to "let go and let God," so I did. I gave it all to Him. Every cut and every stitch. And without hesitation, He took it!

TO BE CONTINUED...

POST #19

I felt like a pin cushion. It was a Friday night and I wasn't even scheduled for surgery until Monday. The doctors wanted me to stay in the ICU all the way up until surgery. They needed to keep my blood pressure stable before any thought of fixing my heart.

I was assured that I wouldn't be relaxing in a "room with a view" this weekend. Something really changed in me after arriving there. I was completely preoccupied with the thought of having someone cut open my chest. I couldn't stop thinking about it, and negative visual images relentlessly bombarded my mind. In addition, I was having a major bout with claustrophobia. I kept thinking about being strapped to a table and waking up in the middle of the operation.

I saw something on television where a woman woke up in the middle of her surgery and could see and feel everything that was going on. She couldn't talk, move or communicate at all, but she felt everything like she had never been given anesthesia.

Why did I ever watch that show? I knew logically that this was a rare occurrence, but it still happened, and I couldn't get it out of my mind.

During that time, a nurse came in and told me that I was in need of another CAT Scan.

I just had one at Henry Mayo Hospital and asked why they couldn't just use that image. Well, it seems that when you transfer from one hospital to another, they must re-do all of your previous tests, scans, and X-rays. Why? Just follow the money trail. That's the only answer I could come up with. I had just completed a CAT Scan a few days earlier and the information on that image hadn't changed. Go figure!

POST #20

Claustrophobia

As I was being wheeled down the hallway to the CAT Scan machine, I remembered the previous test. They lay you on a table, put your arms above your head and move you into a tube (kind of like a big donut). I did great the first time around. This round didn't go so well. As I was laying there, I had my arms over my head staring at a little red light approximately six inches above my eyes. The two technicians behind the glass window spoke clearly through a speaker and instructed me to wait for a signal, and upon that signal, I was then to hold my breath and sit very still. That way, they could take the best possible picture of my chest. Ten seconds after those instructions, the room went completely silent and everyone behind the glass window magically disappeared!

No voices, no signals...nothing! I was thinking, *"Okay, someone will be back in a minute to pull me out of here."* Still nothing.

It seemed like I was laying there for about ten minutes, all by myself, and then it happened. Claustrophobia set in! I was inside that big donut, I had my arms over my head and immediately started feeling like I couldn't breathe. I tried desperately to focus on that little light above my face. "Hey, guys, anybody there?" I said firmly, with no response from anyone! Now my wheels were turning and I started to panic! I thought to myself, *"focus, focus!"* I just kept looking at that little red light, knowing I could completely snap at any second. "Is anyone there?" I asked. Again, no response.

Right then, my mind traveled back to when I was about nine or ten. My brothers and I were playing hide and seek in the basement and I had the brilliant idea of hiding in the laundry hamper. It was one of those clothes bins with a flip up lid.

Eventually I was found, but instead of just tagging me, my older brother thought it would be funny to sit on top of that lid while I screamed for him to let me out. I'm sure it was just a minute or so, but in my mind, it felt like an eternity!

I will always remember pleading with my brother over and over. Begging him to let me out, as he laughed harder with every cry for help.

That was my first and only experience with claustrophobia and I hadn't thought about it in years. Now, I'm reliving that same experience all over again.

"Jesus, please get me out of here", as my mind raced! Every ounce of focus I could muster was on that little red light as I continued to pray. Just then, reminiscent of my brother finally lifting the lid to that laundry hamper, someone finally walked back into the room. "Sorry, Mr. Fridlund. I got sidetracked there for a moment." He said apologetically. "Just hurry and get me out of here," I said with shortness of breath.

I was being freed from this experience but by then my mind and emotions were all jacked up. All I kept thinking was, "*I only have until Monday to figure out how I'm gonna get out of this operation.*"

TO BE CONTINUED...

POST #21

I was back in the ICU. I had two days before my heart surgery, and I was very nervous. What I went through since arriving at UCLA, really took a toll on my psyche. As a man, I liked to think of myself as mentally tough, but given enough time and the right circumstances, anyone can be broken. I was no exception.

Every time I would dwell on my fast approaching operation, My mind would be overwhelmed with claustrophobic thoughts. It was very difficult to calm my mind. I remembered how well prayer worked back at the other hospital, so I started praying even more intensely. I pulled out my iPad and played some praise music, closed my eyes and started telling God how much I needed Him. I laid it out. I basically told Him what He already knew, what I was afraid of, all my concerns and fears, and then after a few minutes, I started to believe that He would take care of me like He always had.

Then, it hit me! What could be the worst possible outcome? I might die on the operating table?

"That's it!" I thought. *"If I die during surgery, wouldn't I be in heaven with Jesus?" "Isn't that like being given a free vacation to Hawaii? Not a bad consolation prize!"* I thought to myself. The second that became a realization, those negative feelings began to be replaced with the joy and the peace I was given days earlier at Henry Mayo Hospital. It was gradual, but by the next morning, I was completely recharged!

I learned that receiving God's peace, regardless of the situation I was facing, was always a result of my being proactive. In other words, if I didn't cry out to Him and reach out my hand first, He wouldn't be able to pull me out of the pit. I would still be clawing my way through the dark, without direction, and alone.

I'm a real slow learner (just ask my wife), but I now understand that God is the Father and I will always be the child. I'm also convinced that God's number one desire in life is to be part of ours.

TO BE CONTINUED...

POST #22

The weekend passed and Monday morning arrived. The day of my operation was upon me! I felt pretty good. No worries, no stress. I was even joking around with the staff. My only concern was if my wife (with traffic) would arrive before I went into surgery. It was touch and go, but she made it and was able to walk alongside my bed as I was wheeled down the hallway to the operating room. I wasn't even nervous. To be honest, I was relieved. The whole ordeal had been such a long process, and I was pretty exhausted. The thought of being put to sleep for a little while seemed somewhat inviting.

I mentioned to my wife earlier that when I was praying, I had asked Jesus about going to Heaven for a visit. I found out through some research that during open heart surgery the patient is given medicine that stops the heartbeat once they're connected to the heart-lung bypass machine. The heart actually has no blood pumping through it during the operation (that way the Surgeon can make the necessary repairs), so technically, I'm heartless!

Well, I just figured since my heart was stopping for a while, I would be a good candidate to visit Heaven, even if it was the result of a technicality. My wife just laughed, but I was dead serious!...excuse the pun. Putting that aside, I prayed with Robynn (that I actually would come back) and kissed her goodbye at the entrance of the "OR," just in case. Then they wheeled me in. The first thing I noticed was how cold the room was. It was like a walk-in refrigerator! Oh my gosh, it was freezing! I actually felt sorry for the operating staff. I can't imagine spending seven hours in that room trying to operate with frozen hands. Tough job! They moved me from my warm bed to a cold metal slab (still wrapped in my blankets) and then we just hung out, talking for a few minutes. I met everybody. They told me about each one of their jobs and what they would be doing. The atmosphere was very casual and relaxed. Now, here's where it got kinda weird. One of the nurses told me that the anesthesiologist was running late, but when he arrived he would explain the procedure, then lull me into a "twilight sleep" before he put me under. "Okay, sounds great," I said, and that was the last thing that I remember.

TO BE CONTINUED...

POST #23

I wanna see Heaven

The surgery was underway. I was completely asleep and don't remember dreaming at all. Before I went under, I prayed, and again had only one request. That I visit Heaven!

That was the foremost thought on my mind. I had prayed and prayed for this since I was a little kid and I knew that at some point in the operation, they'd have to unplug my heart. This was my big chance, and I was going for it!

The following is a true account of what happened to me during that surgery:

Throughout the entire operation, I never once had a sense of being in a dream state. If I did dream, I certainly didn't remember a thing. What I do remember very clearly was being outside of my body. I wasn't floating overhead watching the doctors operate on me or anything of that nature. I was actually floating in space. I knew it was space (as we know it) because I moved my head all around to investigate and realized that everywhere I looked, there were stars. Countless stars. The atmosphere was warm and peaceful. Immediately, I realized I was in a very safe place.

Understand, like most people, I dream when I sleep. Sometimes they seem so real, but there's always an obvious indication during the dream or after waking up, that it was still just a dream. An example of this would be, you're driving down the street in your car and talking to your friend who's sitting in the passenger seat next to you. It all seems very normal and real, until you look again and notice that he's a purple bunny wearing a tux and smoking a cigar. There will always be some indication that you were dreaming. Something that's just slightly off. During this experience though, I had no indication at all that it was a dream. I've analyzed it over and over and I'm fully convinced it was a real experience.

Getting on with my story, there I was, floating in space. I knew I wasn't alone. I knew that Jesus was "somewhere close." After what seemed like a few minutes, I called out, "Jesus, are you there?" It was kind of a weird question to ask, because I knew He was. I felt His presence all around me. It was like a newborn baby that knows his Mother is close by. He just knows!

There was no answer though. "I know you're there, Jesus." I said. "I just want to see Heaven. Even for just a minute." I heard no response. I asked again, this time a little more forcefully. Still nothing!

Just then, Jesus spoke to me. It was like a friend leaning in to tell you a secret. I could almost feel His breath as He spoke into my right ear.

His voice was calm, caring and completely familiar. "It's not your time," He said. The second He said those words, a screen appeared in front of me. It was huge, spanning across all that I could see. I guess the best way to describe it is to imagine the largest computer screen you have ever seen in your life and multiply it by a billion (and I'm sure that still wouldn't come close). I was looking at this massive screen and thinking, *"what the heck?"*

All of a sudden, letters started to appear, forming words right in front of me, in the most amazing pink color you could ever imagine. My eyes scanned the heavens as full sentences were formed:

I HAVE GIVEN YOU THE PERFECT WIFE!

I HAVE GIVEN YOU THE PERFECT FAMILY!

I HAVE GIVEN YOU THE PERFECT PURPOSE!

The letters were so brilliant, I had to squint! I remember reading it over and over again. I knew the Lord kept it very simple, so I wouldn't forget it! Seconds later, I was back in the ICU. I was alert, focused and in no pain whatsoever. The first thing out of my mouth was, "Seriously Lord? You're putting me back in my body? Thanks a lot!" I said sarcastically. Was I upset? Not really. It would have been cool to see Heaven, but I think Jesus had something more important for me to see.

TO BE CONTINUED...

POST #24

I was back in my body and feeling good. I arrived in the operating room about 8:00 am and was wheeled out of there about 4:30 pm. It took about seven and a half hours to complete the surgery. I can't even believe the concentration these doctors must have to pull off something like that. I guess that's why they make the big bucks!

I was taken back to the ICU and didn't wake up until after midnight.

I feared waking up prematurely with a tube down my throat, so, I asked God before the operation to keep me under until they pulled that tube out. Well, he honored that request and woke me up after all the dirty work was done.

After giving Jesus a bad time for not taking me to Heaven, I remember asking the night nurse for some water and then passed out for another eight or nine hours. The next morning they didn't waste any time getting me up and mobile. I was walking, not very far, but walking. I was also on a lot of pain medication. OxyContin, Vicodin, etc.

The first two days out of surgery were very foggy. I felt like Rocky Balboa after his match with Apollo Creed. My eyes felt like they were swollen shut and I was completely out of it.

People would tell me before the operation how great the drugs were and how much I would be enjoying myself during the recovery stage. That was not the case at all! I hated it! I couldn't talk, I was having hallucinations, and I was sick to my stomach the entire time. It was horrible! After two days, all I wanted was to get off all pain medications. They looked at me like I was crazy. Well, from that point forward, I refused to take anything but Tylenol and I can honestly say that I had almost no pain, anywhere! My chest was ripped open no more than 48 hours earlier, and all I needed for pain was a couple of Tylenol? Thank you, Jesus!

Although it may seem like a great endorsement for Tylenol, Jesus gets all the credit!

I spent several more days recovering in the ICU. Each day was a new lesson.

I learned a lot about myself, my God and my purpose in this world. I know that sounds corny, but it's true! I was given a rare opportunity that most people never receive, in which I was able to do nothing but reflect. Reflect on my life, my relationships and my Creator. As the days slowly passed, one truth played over and over in my mind. "It's not about me!" Sometimes I felt like God was screaming in my ear, "It's not about you, Dave! It's not about you!"

I cried so much in that ICU that most days I was dehydrated. God was working on me and I had nowhere to hide. The "white noise" of life does not exist in the ICU. It was a strange calm in that room. Most of the time, it was so quiet that the only thing I could hear were my thoughts...and God's voice.

But, I think the most important thing of all, was knowing that I couldn't get up and leave. I was stuck there and that's exactly what God wanted. He wanted to reach me at all cost.

All in all, I spent a total of nine days in the ICU. It was the most painful, humiliating, and debilitating time of my life. I highly recommend it!

POST #25

Fathers Day

The day finally came. I was being transferred from Intensive Care to a regular hospital room! God really broke me down in the ICU, and quite frankly, I was in need of a break. A "room with a view" was just what the doctor ordered!

When I arrived at my room, I was blown away. It was beautiful, and all mine! I was still on the 7th Floor (how appropriate) but this time I was overlooking the entire city of Westwood. I could see the cafes, movie theaters and more importantly, the sun! The room was facing East and had a long bench right in front of the window, so I could enjoy the sunrise in the mornings. I can't even tell you how much that would mean to me over those next few days. The ICU would only allow two visitors at a time, so I was never able to see my whole family at once. My goal was to hopefully be discharged by June 21st, which was Father's Day. It became pretty obvious though, that I was going to overshoot that date, but at least I was going to be in that beautiful room on Fathers Day, and I expected my whole family to join in on the party!

By that time, I had most of the tubes and wires pulled out of me, so I felt pretty free. I still had an IV in my arm at all times, but that was livable. It was a pain in the butt when I needed to go to the bathroom (oh, I also had my own bathroom. Yay!) but livable.

The overall feeling I had when I arrived in that room was complete appreciation for everything! I was just so happy to be there. To be out of ICU was such an emotional high, I literally didn't know what to do with myself. I had been so broken down over those last nine days that I felt like a piece of putty. I would find out just how broken I truly was later that afternoon...when my whole family would gather in my room to honor "yours truly."

A few hours later, I was waking up from a little nap when I heard a knock on the door. It was one of my kids, presents in hand, followed by the rest of my family. As they each entered the room, I began tearing up. I was like a little ole' grandma, sitting there waiting for someone to visit. It was awesome! They brought me treats, presents, and wonderful handwritten cards. Oh, those cards!

In the past, when my kids would present their Fathers Day cards to me, I would read them out loud and tell each one how much I appreciated the effort they put in to writing them. Well, today would be a much different experience for all of us!

As I started to read the first card, I got about two words into it and I broke down in tears. I wiped my eyes and started reading again. I got two more words out and broke down again. My kids were looking at me like I was crazy! I had to finally put the card down because I couldn't see the words through the tears. It was hilarious! I tried another card and the same thing happened. I was laughing and crying at the same time. My daughter bought me a $20 Jamba Juice gift card, and when I saw it, I just broke down again, balling like a baby...I was so happy! I was crying my eyes out and my kids were cracking up every time I did!

The man my wife and children encountered that day, was one they'd never met.

The remainder of my stay in the hospital was like that, every single day! Nurses would come into my room to take blood or give me a pill, and my eyes would start welling up with tears all over again. It was crazy! Everyone seemed to like the new Dave. Even I noticed the difference.

The early morning, between 5:30 and 7:00 am was my favorite part of the day. I would sit by that window, play worship music, talk to God, and of course, bawl my eyes out!

Never in my life had I ever felt that close to God. I didn't want it to stop. I was overwhelmed with God's love every minute and it spilled out of me to everyone I came in contact with. Literally! Doctors, nurses, staff and even the cleaning crew noticed it. It was the first time I ever felt God completely using me to touch others with His love.

There was this young nurse who came to draw my blood one afternoon. She attempted five different times, stabbing my veins over and over again and apologizing every time she did. I was so filled with love and appreciation for her, that I couldn't care less how many times she poked me, I just kept praising her and telling her how special she was for wanting to help people. I know she was touched.

God showed me very clearly that His desire is to touch broken people, and He wants to use His children to do it. The problem is, most of us are not broken ourselves. I know I wasn't. God said to Paul, *"My grace is sufficient for you, for My power is made perfect in weakness" (2 Corinthians 12:9-10).*

In other words, when we're completely broken and in need of God's love just to get us through the day, then and only then, are we in a position to let God love people through us.

My whole life I thought I followed Jesus. I was wrong. It's not about going to church or living by a set of rules and it's certainly not about having theological depth, or receiving great revelation from or about God. It's much simpler. It's about having a desperate reliance on Jesus. The way a drowning man gasps for air.

I spent a total of 20 days and nights in two different hospitals. Each day I relied less on me and more on Him, until Jesus was all I needed or wanted.

That was my experience, customized for me alone, and a defining moment in my life that I hoped would never end.

POST #26

My new job

After many weeks of rest and recovery at home, my doctor gave me the okay to go back to work on a very limited, part time basis, and I was excited to start my new job. I would be traveling all around the country with a company that conducts seminars teaching real estate investing. I wasn't sure I was ready, but I knew one thing; I couldn't sit around any longer. I was going crazy at home, so I hit the road!

August, 2015

It took every ounce of energy I had to keep up the pace my new position demanded. I was on the road for about five days a week. I'd fly home for a day or two and then get right back on an airplane. It was grueling. I didn't want anyone to know how hard it was on me physically, but we needed the money and I needed the satisfaction of knowing that I was contributing. On the road, I could fake it pretty well, or so I thought.

I'd arrive back at my hotel at the end of an event and just collapse. I'd wake up the next morning still in my work clothes, somehow make it through a shower, and by the time I got down to the lobby, I'd pretend to be as enthusiastic as possible.

One morning, I was so exhausted that I almost collapsed in the elevator as I was going down to the lobby for breakfast. When the doors opened and I'd notice my co-workers standing there, I would quickly compose myself, put on a big energetic smile and pretend like I was pumped to start my day. "Don't ever let them see you sweat!" as the saying goes. I remember thinking, *"Smile, just get through this day,"* all the while feeling like I was a hundred-year-old man that just got run over by a truck.

Unfortunately, that would be my life for the next fourteen months.

Breathing on my own

October, 2016

A year passed and my body was recovering well. I had my share of challenges, but I was earning a living. Between my wife's salary and mine, we were doing pretty well. Some might even say we were thriving. My life was getting back to "normal". My wife was happy, my kids were enjoying life and we lacked for nothing. Not only that, we were involved in a great local church that we absolutely loved, and we built some wonderful relationships through the congregation. But, something was wrong, and I couldn't put my finger on it. I knew one thing for sure, I wasn't very happy.

Several months passed and I still seemed to be going through the motions of life. There was nothing out of the "norm," and that was precisely the problem. It was TOO normal! I would get up at the same time every morning, I would listen to praise music, read my Bible, and then pray. I would then try to be a "good Christian" the rest of the day, only to start the same process over and over again each morning.

One night, change finally came. A change that would shake me to my core!

I was on a business trip in a hotel room in Huntsville, Alabama. I awoke from a deep sleep and just happened to look at the alarm clock next to the bed. It was exactly 3:00 am. I remember being stricken with grief. I felt like someone close to me had just died. Immediately, I tried to recall if I had just dreamt about someone dying. It was one of those dreams where the emotions stay with you even after you wake up. I just remember how desperate I felt at that moment. I got up, knelt at the end of my bed and began to pray, asking God to do something in my life. I longed for the relationship I had with Jesus back in the hospital. I was desperate again! I blurted out, "Do whatever it takes to bring me back to you, Jesus!" I didn't care about anything at that moment. I just kept repeating, "Whatever it takes God, whatever it takes!" At the time, I was unaware of the cost of that request. I only knew I was willing to pay it.

POST #27

November 2016

Road trip!!

The Big day was here! After many weeks of talking about it, my wife and I were finally heading to Vegas for our good friends' wedding. While everyone else was staying at Caesars Palace, my wife and I decided to use some of the Hilton points I earned from my job to stay down the street at the Embassy Suites.

We were running a bit late and Robynn was concerned about being on time to a show she had booked for us and another couple that evening. My wife grew up with one of the headliners of the show and was able to use her connections to put together a pretty memorable evening. There was only one problem. I was starting to get a fever!

We passed the Nevada State-Line, so I knew Las Vegas was not far away. My wife was glued to her watch as she tried to figure out the fastest route to our hotel, and then back down the Vegas strip to the show.

I, on the other hand, was driving as fast as I could, as my fever turned to nausea.

"We're finally here! Just two more exits and I'll be headed to my bed!" I thought to myself. Unfortunately, my stomach wasn't going to wait that long. I quickly pulled over to the shoulder, and with cars speeding by and in the middle of rush hour traffic, I threw open my

drivers side door and proceeded to hurl. My wife like-wise insisted that my last stop for the evening would be straight to our hotel room and bed! We both felt pretty confident that I had the flu.

We finally arrived at the Embassy Suites, and with heavy eyes I wheeled my bag through the lobby. "*If I can just make it to my room*," I thought. "*Then, everything will be fine.*" I figured I would gracefully bow out for the evening and catch the wedding ceremony the next afternoon. Nobody would even miss me.

As you will soon find out, that option was never in the cards!

So, we arrived at our hotel room, I went straight to bed and got under the covers. Since I had thrown up earlier, my stomach was feeling much better. My wife was hurrying to get ready as I was trying to position myself to be as comfortable as possible. I knew I had a fairly high fever and was preparing to ride it out. My wife checked on me one last time and hurried out the door to her Uber. I would visit the toilet several more times before her return.

Later that night, I believe it was around 11:00 pm. I heard the hotel door open. It was Robynn. I had been throwing up since I arrived and was beginning to dry heave. She returned from her evening event and checked on me one last time, while preparing for bed. I would have no memory of what my wife would see or encounter over the next one and a half days.

The only way for anyone to truly understand the gravity of what was to come would be to hear and see the rest of the story through two pairs of eyes; my wife Robynn's, and my own.

Through Robynn's eyes:

After the show, I returned to the hotel room. I had one dose of Nyquil in my purse which I gave to Dave. It was enough to help him feel better, and we both slept through the night. The next morning we went down to the breakfast buffet. Dave was not that hungry, but still managed to get down a little something. We had plenty of time before the wedding, and decided to get back into bed for a while. I needed a nap and Dave was still unsure if he would be feeling well enough to make the wedding. We laid in bed the rest of the morning, and although we occasionally nodded off, we were able to make it through a movie. As the day progressed, it was evident that he was not feeling any better, so we decided that I should go to the wedding alone. While it was disappointing, at least I could represent the two of us.

As I left for the night, I let Dave know that I would check in with him as the evening progressed. The ceremony was beautiful, and I even shot some video of everyone telling my husband, "Get well! Wish you were here!" As the night was wrapping up, I called Dave to see if I could pick up anything for him on my way back. He asked for more cold &

flu medication, so I had to move fast to find a place that would sell meds at that time of night. I brought Dave's medication back to the hotel room, and we both settled down for what we hoped would be a good night's sleep. Little did we know, that would be the calm before the storm.

POST #28

When all hell broke loose

Through Dave's eyes:

At one point, I recall getting out of bed. I was thirsty, and knew we had bottled water in the mini fridge. I walked from the bedroom to the small living area, about twenty feet away. It felt like the air conditioning was on full blast. The closer I moved to the living room, the colder it got. I knew where I was, I could tell it was a hotel room, my hotel room, but somehow it seemed different. The atmosphere had changed. I remember thinking, "I've gotta get back to bed, back to my wife. I felt safe there. I was only a few feet away, but it seemed like miles.

I opened the refrigerator door, pulled out my water and turned to close the door.

Then it happened. There they were, inches from my face. Two of them, and at least eight to nine feet tall. I was frozen with fear. Not like the superficial fear you experience while watching a horror movie, but an all consuming, all encompassing fear, completely devoid of any hope or consolation. I was completely vulnerable, with nowhere to escape! I wanted to wake up my wife to warn her. I tried to scream, but I couldn't even speak. One of them grabbed my throat and started choking me while the other was screaming, "You're dead! We're gonna kill you!" "You're dead!"

Immediately, I knew that these were not hallucinations or figments of my imagination. They were real, they were demons, and they were there for a purpose. Looking back on that experience, I can now write about it from a distance, but at the time, I can assure you that I was scared out of my mind. The grip around my neck kept getting tighter and I wasn't able to breathe. I was suffocating, and yelling for help became impossible. As a last resort, I was able to form my lips and say, "Jesus!" in what sounded like a half whisper.

The second, and I mean the second I whispered that Name, the crippling fear that had consumed my whole body was instantly gone. Even the atmosphere had changed. I was still staring at those demons, but I realized at that moment that something was drastically different. They were the ones that were terrified! The larger of the two released my throat and began backing away, along with the loudmouth, who was screaming at me earlier and pronouncing my death. *"What's happening, what are they so afraid of,"* I thought. Then it hit me. *"They are afraid of me!"*

Right then, I was filled with the power and boldness of a lion! *"I could take on the world and everything in it!"* I thought. And I wanted to start with those two! As I began moving toward them, reinforcements supernaturally appeared. They were literally coming out of the walls. Big ones, little ones, each demon more menacing than the last.

Like a gang, they were all standing back, huddling, like they were strategizing their attack. But the funny thing was that I had absolutely no fear! At that exact second, I felt a presence over my right shoulder. When I glanced back, I saw the largest man I'd ever seen. He was about eight feet tall with long flowing hair and completely ripped from head to toe. I immediately knew he was an angel. It was awesome!

There he stood, full of confidence and looking at me as if to say, "You ready to do this?" Suddenly, in his hand appeared a giant golden sword! Before I could even blink, there were demons flying everywhere. With a wave of his sword, they were being thrown across the room and smashing into walls. It made an MMA match look like childsplay. Several demons tried to escape, but he kept pulling them back. I was having a blast! Every punch I landed felt amazing! This wasn't a fight; it was a thrashing! The angel was teaching them a lesson, and allowing me to join in. It was fast, devastating, and in the blink of an eye, it was over...and I found myself lying in a hospital bed.

POST #29

Through Robynn's eyes:

Dave was restless. He got out of bed and went to the bathroom several times that night feeling sick. I stayed up as long as I could, but eventually fell asleep myself. It wasn't until about five o'clock in the morning that I heard him say something from outside our bedroom. I got out of bed and walked into the living room.

There was Dave, standing straight up, facing the bedroom. His eyes were wide open and his body was stiff and rigid. His arms were straight down at his sides and his hands were shaking uncontrollably. "David, what's wrong?" I asked. He didn't answer me. He just stood there, looking straight ahead. Then, I heard him say in a very methodical voice, "So, this is how it's gonna happen?" I tried to get through to him again, but he was completely unresponsive. He then said, "Bring it on!"

I tried to get him to sit down but he would not move. I ran to the phone and dialed the front desk. I told them I needed an ambulance immediately. Then, suddenly, he started walking toward the bedroom and stood next to the bed with his back facing the wall. Within the next couple of minutes, his body slowly lowered itself, like a plank, face down on the bed. By then, the manager had let herself in our hotel room and joined me in the bedroom. I had been praying through the whole process, but had to talk to the paramedics on the phone while the manager stayed with him, in an attempt to get Dave to respond to her.

When I came back, she joined me in prayer. In addition to everything else that was going on with my husband, we were also concerned about him suffocating on the bed, so we grabbed him and rolled him over onto his back. His body slid down onto the floor. I was kneeling next to him when the manager left the bedroom to let in the paramedics. I grabbed Dave and immediately began to pray, "I bind you Satan, in the name of Jesus, you can't have my husband! You have no right to him! He is a child of God!" That's when the paramedics showed up and took over.

POST #30

Through Robynn's eyes:

The ambulance attendants loaded Dave up, and I was able to follow him in the fire truck. When we arrived at the hospital, they rushed Dave into the emergency room. He was unconscious and on life support. It was about 6:00 AM, and over the next several hours he was given a number of tests and scans. I knew that he was sick, but had no idea how close to death he really was. Initially, I was told that

Dave had a brain hemorrhage. It was soon after that I was given the news that his organs were shutting down. It would take the next 24 hours before we would find out whether or not he was going to survive, and if he did, there would be a good possibility he would suffer permanent brain damage due to the hemorrhage.

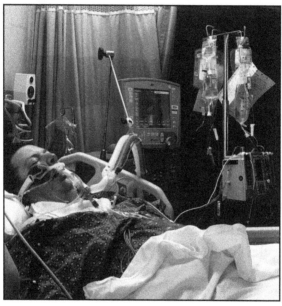

There I was, in a hospital, all by myself, and feeling very alone. My husband was dying, and all I knew to do was to get on the phone with family and friends, and post an urgent request for prayer on Facebook. Within an hour, many were responding to my post. I knew then that God's ears were burning!

People really rallied on behalf of Dave. Within three hours of being in that hospital, two close friends that lived in the area came to pray, as well as a pastor of a local church in Vegas. He was asked to come to the hospital through a connection from our home church back in California, and he stayed and prayed through Dave's transition from the emergency room to the ICU. I was both blessed and amazed at how fast people mobilized during this time of crisis.

POST #31

"My Lord my God"

Through Dave's eyes:

I opened my eyes and looked around the room. I could tell where I was. It was quiet, peaceful, and it felt warm and safe. It appeared to be a hospital room, but without a doctor or nurse in site, or anyone else for that matter.

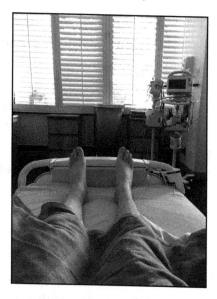

I remember thinking to myself, *"For being in a hospital, I sure do feel great!"*

I felt like I was eighteen again and a world class athlete!

Appearing out of nowhere, I saw Jesus sitting at the end of my bed. As our eyes met, everything else seemed to fade off into the distance. As I looked at Him, He appeared relaxed and content, like He had nowhere to be and all the time in the world to get there. Being with Him was so natural. I didn't feel like I had to do or say anything. It was like being home. I just belonged.

His face was the picture of peace, and behind Him shined the soft glow of His eternal Glory. It was timeless, and painted with colors I hadn't ever imagined. I immediately blurted out, "Let me go!" referring to Heaven. He just looked at me and calmly said, "no buddy."

I asked again, this time pleading my case, "What if I go for a little while, just long enough to see my Grandparents and Mother-in-law?" Again, the answer was "no."

Funny thing, I remember thinking to myself, *"If I can just run around Him before He can grab me, I can probably make it to Heaven!"*

I ran track in college and always thought I was pretty fast back then. But when I attempted to jump out of that bed and run past Him, I shouldn't have been so surprised when He effortlessly caught me. After all, He was Jesus! He was clearly humoring me up to that point and I could tell it was time to listen up! He leaned His whole body toward me, and with a straight face, whispered in my right ear, "We have too much to do!" And with those words, I came back from reality.

POST #32

Through Robynn's eyes:

I was in the room with a nurse as we were trying to get Dave to respond. All of a sudden, he began to thrash around in his bed. We called for help as we had to hold Dave down to insure he wouldn't pull out any vital tubes keeping him alive. He was still on life support, when all of a sudden he began "literally" running in place, kind of like the bicycle exercise you do when you are laying on your back. The nurses and I all started laughing as I said, "Where's he trying to go?" It took several nurses holding Dave down before he finally became calm.

POST #33

Back from reality

Through Dave's eyes:

"Mister Fridlund!...Mister Fridlund! Can you hear me?" *"Who is this woman and why is she in my face?"* I thought. She was so loud, I was really tempted to hold up my middle finger instead of my thumb. But I managed to restrain myself as I nodded and gave her the thumbs up. There were so many tubes coming out of me, I figured I had better be compliant. I remember being really ticked that I was back in my body and back to the grind of this world. The peace that I was experiencing with Jesus came to a crashing halt!

I've come to explain it like this: It was like sitting in a big stuffed chair in front of a blazing fireplace, drinking a cup of hot chocolate one minute, and "POOF!" The next thing you know, you're standing outside in a snowstorm, buck naked. *"Wow! back from reality!"* I thought.

Looking around the room, I saw plenty of busy people. I saw my wife, next to the obnoxious nurse. The smile on her face told me I had all my limbs. I had a breathing tube coming out of my mouth, but was fully aware of my surroundings. There were several voices telling me to relax. My mind was going a mile a minute, trying to figure out where I was, how I got there, and whether or not it was day or night. Heck, I didn't even know what state I was in! The mind is a funny thing. It thrives on information. Every time I tried to ask a question, I was told to relax. Probably because of the breathing tube protruding out of my throat. All I knew was that I was alive, my wife was next to me, and that was good enough for the time being!

POST #34

In the beginning of my recovery, the days were filled with medical tests, scans, and luke warm green jello. I was amazed at how many people came to see me. It wasn't like traveling right around the corner for most of the friends and family who came to visit. This was Vegas! I was humbled with the knowledge of how many people cared. I was also immensely impacted by the thought of how close I came to dying. Being back among "the living," the appreciation I felt for other people was supernatural to say the least! The love that I felt from Jesus was overwhelming, and when I woke up, it seemed to flow out of me effortlessly to everyone around! It didn't matter if it was the guy who was there to pick up the trash; when I would look at him, I could see him for who he was in God's eyes..

The compassion and love I had for people was off the charts! I remember I saw a lady walking down the hallway just outside my door, and my heart broke for her. I found myself praying for her without even knowing why. It was like I felt what Jesus felt, and I saw people through His eyes and not my own. My heart literally broke for that lady, and I didn't know the first thing about her! I was taught growing up and always believed that Jesus lived in my heart, but to actually experience and feel it like I did, went way beyond any sermon, Sunday School lesson or head knowledge I acquired throughout the years. I was experiencing raw compassion and unconditional love for anyone and everyone I came in contact with. It was better than any drug they could have given me. *"If this is the pay-off,"* I thought, *"then it's worth everything I have to go through!"*

What I couldn't see at the time, was the mental battle that was ahead of me.

POST #35

The Dread

It was about a week after I woke up that I started experiencing the attacks. They came on quickly and without notice. I remember lying in bed, feeling fine, and suddenly, just like back in the hotel room, the room went dim and a wave of cold air washed over me.

I immediately felt a dark presence, like the devil himself was hovering over my bed.

It was hard to explain. It felt like death. It felt like God had left the world. All I wanted to do was curl up and die. It was quite a departure from the high I was feeling just moments ago. I experienced that feeling several times throughout the day before I was finally able to explain it to my wife. I called it, "The Dread". It escalated in frequency and intensity as time progressed. I felt like I was going out of my mind! I needed my wife next to me at all times. If she even hinted about leaving the room, I would freak out! The "Dread" would hit me so often that I couldn't stand to be by myself for even a moment. I needed her prayers. I needed her to talk me down from the ledge and bring me back. It was debilitating. Never in my life had I felt this kind of hopelessness, and I knew I couldn't battle this on my own. During the attacks, I would beg God to help me. I started speaking out loud to the devil, telling him to get out of my room and out of my mind. I'm sure I looked and sounded insane. I didn't care! With every attack, I felt like I was dying and being dragged to hell. Just recalling those initial attacks sends chills up and down my spine as I write this post. All I can say is, "God is Great!! The devil is a punk, and thank you Lord for patient wives that pray!"

POST #36

The "Dread" continued all the way up to the day I finally left Sunrise Hospital. I was told by the doctors and nurses on staff that the attacks on my mind were PTSD (Post Traumatic Stress Disorder). At the time, I didn't understand what was happening to me, but in hindsight, it all makes perfect sense. The mind is a complicated thing, and I have developed great understanding and compassion for returning vets and head trauma victims who have been afflicted with this disorder.

The excitement was hard to contain, as my wife filled out the discharge paperwork. I couldn't get out of there fast enough. Every time I heard a curtain divider slide open or close, I would start having another panic attack. Little things would trigger it!

Like I stated earlier, the mind is a complicated thing. But I wasn't letting anything slow me down from getting out of that hospital that day!

As I was sitting on the end of my bed, waiting patiently for the green light, the Doctor who was in charge of my case stopped by my room to say goodbye. He was a small, middle-aged, Indian man. I thanked him for all he had done for me and told him how much I appreciated his staff. Before we parted, he said the most remarkable thing to me. "Over the years, I've seen many people come though our hospital, but not many have recovered as fully and rapidly as you have considering the seriousness and nature of your particular stroke. Sir, you should not have even survived the ambulance ride!" he said, shaking his head. He went on to say, "Mr. Fridlund, in the twenty years I've been an ER Doctor, I've never seen what I would consider to be a miracle. But, from this point forward, if someone ever asks me, you, Sir, would be that miracle!" I was speechless. Not only had Jesus made himself known to me in a way that I could never have imagined, but he had touched many in that hospital. Especially that humble Doctor. I pray every day that God will continue to make Himself known to doctors and nurses in hospitals everywhere. Many people don't believe that Jesus still performs miracles today. My answer to them is, and will always be, "If you don't believe me, just ask my doctor."

POST #37

Leaving Las Vegas

The sun was warm on my face as the nurse wheeled me out of the hospital. I was so happy to see our car and even more happy to get in and drive off! As we pulled out, all that was on my mind was finding the interstate and heading home. "We have one stop before we leave," my wife said.

She had purchased a card and some flowers for the hotel manager at the Embassy Suites. This woman had done so much for us, and my wife just wanted to thank her and give me a chance to do the same. The only problem was we had to drive back to the hotel and walk back into the lobby to see her! Just the thought of driving by that hotel, let alone walking inside gave me the chills and prompted me to experience those feelings of anxiety all over again. The closer we got, the more my mind raced. As we pulled into the parking lot, I finally gave up fighting it and went into a full-on panic attack.

Several minutes later, the attack decreased enough for me to run in and thank that wonderful woman. I remember getting out of the car and walking to the lobby, but nothing after that. My wife said the manager enjoyed seeing and hugging me, but it must have been too traumatic for my mind to remember.

A year later I went back to that hotel. My company was doing an event in Las Vegas, and reserved a ball-room in that same Embassy Suites.

I had a second chance to thank her and give her another big hug; one that I would always remember!

I walked up to the reservation desk and asked to speak with the manager. When she came to the counter, I asked if she remembered me. The minute I said that, she jumped up, ran around the counter and threw her arms around me! I must have left quite an impression during our last encounter. Turns out, she's an amazing Christian woman who loves Jesus with all her heart. "You saved my life that morning," I said. She looked at me with tears in her eyes and said, "It wasn't me that saved your life."

That confirmed it! God had all the right people set in place that night. It was the perfect storm; orchestrated by design, and He knew in the end, His Son would get the glory!

"And we know that all things work together for good to them that love God and are called according to His purpose". (Romans 8:28)

POST #38

My first day home

The first morning home I intended on sleeping in, but decided to get up with my wife and tag along as she drove the kids to school. Back at the hospital, I'd been getting up between 5:30 and 6:00 am every morning to pray. I didn't want to lose the intimacy I had established with Jesus up until that point. I had a few minutes, so I jumped in the shower. The best thing about taking a shower, in my experience, is that God, like clockwork, almost always speaks to me during those times. Don't ask me why, but we evidently share the same love for water!

On that particular morning, though, something was wrong. I immediately started grieving in my heart. I was dwelling on how quickly I grew apart from the Lord in such a short amount of time after my open heart surgery, just a year and a half earlier. I don't know why I started thinking so intensely about it, but I found myself begging God not to leave me and to continue living through me. To this day, it's hard to explain how desperate I felt in my heart. I just remember begging Him to forgive me, to never leave me, and to fill me again with His presence. I kept saying, "I don't want to be normal, Lord, I don't want to go back to how I've always been. Please Jesus, I don't want to be normal."

In the midst of begging and pleading and while tears and hot water were running down my face, Jesus spoke to me! It wasn't an audible voice. It was what the Bible calls "a still, small voice," and it was as clear as a bell.

Just then, I began to bubble over with Joy!! It wasn't a natural, emotional joy that most people experience. I wasn't just emotionally happy, but I was experiencing a supernatural presence of His Spirit that the Bible describes as "Joy unspeakable and full of Glory," and it quickly filled the shower. My heart was overflowing with His love, and it was amazing! It wasn't just amazing; it was awesomely amazing!!

As I write this, I'm actually getting filled with Joy just thinking about it!

By now, you are probably wondering what Jesus said to me in that shower.

Well, He said, "Welcome to your new normal!"

POST #39

My new normal

After my encounter with God in the shower, I decided to make it a habit to get up with my wife and take my kids to school. Because of the stroke, I was not allowed to drive. This was actually not a problem for me, as I never minded being a passenger.

We were running late one morning, as usual, and trying to get out of the house as fast as we could. Robynn was driving, I was in the passenger seat, and my kids were in the back. There are a couple of ways to get to our kids' school, but the route my wife chose to take that morning would be life changing. She decided it would be faster to get off the main streets and cut through a neighborhood that led to the school.

We were making good time as we approached a stop sign at a four-way intersection. Just as my wife was slowing down, we heard a bang!

My wife yelled, "Oh, my gosh! That lady just got hit by a car!"

As my wife tells it, suddenly, our passenger door flew open and she saw me jump out of the car and start running–full speed–to the lady laying in the street. At the time, I wasn't thinking of how I was just released from the hospital or how I probably shouldn't be sprinting across an intersection. It just happened.

When I looked down at her, my first impression was, she was really hurt. My wife was calling 911 as my mind was racing. Her face swelled before my eyes as a result of the impact from the car that hit her and the asphalt upon which she landed face first. She appeared to be in her early 60's and was bleeding from what looked like shattered eye sockets and a broken nose. She was lying flat on her back, and I knew from what I had learned through my Boy Scout first aid training years ago not to move her until the paramedics arrive. What happened next was as much a surprise to me as everyone else that gathered around.

Without thinking, I just laid down on the wet street right next to her. She was looking straight up at the sky as I leaned in close to her right ear. I remember saying, "Can you feel Him? He's right here! Can you feel him?" In a soft voice, she responded, "Yes!"

I asked her to tell me where it hurt. She pointed to her shoulder. It looked broken, or dislocated at the very least. I gently laid my hand on her shoulder and asked Jesus to take her pain away. Then, I asked her to point to the next area that was hurting. She moved her hand down to her stomach. When she did, I was concerned that she might have internal bleeding. I laid my hand on her stomach and asked Jesus to heal her and take away the pain. The last area she pointed to was her head, and as I hovered my hand over her forehead and eyes, I asked the Lord once again to take away her pain.

I could hear the ambulance approaching, and knew my time was coming to an end. I leaned closer to her right ear and whispered, "In just a little while, you are going to be warm and comfortable in a hospital bed, and you are going to feel like a million bucks! Do you believe me?" She said, "Yes!" I told her that Jesus would be with her the whole time, and that He wasn't going to leave her side.

As the paramedics arrived, I remember hearing myself say, "Don't worry, it's just bumps and bruises. Just bumps and bruises." As they moved her to the stretcher, I kept thinking to myself, *"What was I thinking? This lady might die!"* *"Why would I tell her that all she had were bumps and bruises?"*

Immediately, I started second guessing myself. *"Was I giving her false hope?"*

TO BE CONTINUED....

POST #40

As the ambulance drove off, I thought to myself, *"I don't even know her name."* My wife told me she would find out which hospital the lady was taken to. That whole morning, I continued to pray for her. I wanted her to be ok, but my main prayer was that Jesus would become known to this woman in a greater way than she had known Him before.

Later that afternoon, I received a call from my wife. She had done a little investigating and found out to which hospital the lady had been sent. Robynn also had gone as far as calling the hospital and check on her. Evidently, the woman had told us her name at the scene of the accident, although I have no recollection. My wife used that information to contact her hospital room directly.

When Robynn called, the receptionist immediately patched her into the women's room, and she answered the phone herself! My wife introduced herself and explained who she was and what had happened. She then asked how the woman was feeling, and, in an upbeat voice, she responded, "Wonderful!"

The following is the text I received from my wife:

Dave, She told me she had no recollection of the accident. She wanted to know exactly what had happened. I told her every detail, how my husband prayed with her on the ground and that I called 911. I asked how she was. She said she only had a broken collarbone, a bruised head and face, and no pain whatsoever.

She said she believes that my husbands prayers worked.

God once again got the glory that morning! Not me, not Robynn, not the ambulance driver or anyone at that scene. God moved quickly and decisively, like He always does! If we're sensitive to His Spirit and ready to follow, He'll always let us tag along for the ride!

POST #41

Angels unaware

I'd been home for a while and enjoying my time with Jesus and my family. This morning, however, I woke up very early; even earlier than usual. Something was not sitting right with me and I couldn't put my finger on it. The best way to describe it would be to say that I was sad. I had no idea why, I just knew what I was feeling. As I made my way downstairs to the big red chair where I typically like to start my day, I began to cry. As unnerving as it was, at the same time I felt comforted. Somehow, I knew a foundation was being built. God was trying to prepare me for something, so I rolled with it. I started to pray, and suddenly, fear came over me, like I was stranded on an island, watching the boat leave without me. While praying, I remember blurting out, "I don't want to be a regular Christian, Jesus! I don't want to be average! You need to know that I'm serious and I mean business!" I was crying and begging Him to believe me! I knew Jesus loved me, but I wasn't entirely sure He knew I loved Him. Really loved Him! After a little groveling, I wiped my eyes, picked myself up, and turned on YouTube to watch a sermon and listen to some praise music as I usually did that time of the day. While I was fumbling through the channels, I came across a preacher that I had heard preach a few times prior to my stroke. His name was Paul Washer, and he was speaking to a random group of people somewhere, and these were the words I heard him say:

"There are those of you who aren't satisfied with being an average Christian. You're serious and you mean business!"

My heart literally stopped! Was the Lord really talking to me through the television set? *"Wow! That's pretty cool!" I thought. As the day progressed, I began to think about how that experience was such an "amazing" coincidence. Coincidence or not, I believed God heard my prayer, and that was good enough for me!*

Later that night, around 11:00 PM, my wife asked me, as she often does, to run to the grocery store to pick up a few items. I enjoy shopping at night. It's quiet, relaxing and it gives me time to think as I stroll through the isles. It's my "therapy" of sorts.

When I entered the store, I could see that they were getting ready to close. I knew I had about ten minutes before they'd kick me out, so I gave a head nod to the manager as I grabbed a small cart and headed toward the cereal aisle. They knew me there and usually granted me a little extra time. As I walked through the isles, I realized that I might be the only one in the store, at least as far as I could see. I was used to seeing the same "night-shift" employees, stocking shelves for the next day. But for some reason, I didn't see any that night. After picking up everything on my list, I decided I'd head to the frozen foods aisle and grab some ice cream for my kids. *"They work hard and deserve a treat,"* I thought to myself. When I buy ice cream, I have this habit of reaching to the back of the freezer in search of the most current expiration date. If you've ever eaten old freezer-burnt ice cream, you'd understand.

After digging all the way to the back of the bottom shelf, I finally found what I was looking for and pulled myself out from the freezer. With ice cream in hand, I stood up, closed the glass door, and turned toward my grocery cart.

"Hi," I heard, as I stood face to face with a beautiful young girl. She appeared to be in her early twenties with long black hair and smiling ear-to-ear. "It's you," she said. "Excuse me?" I said nervously, immediately thinking to myself, *"Ok, where are the cameras?"* while at the same time scanning my cart to make sure my phone and wallet were still in sight!

"We were just driving by, and Jesus told me to come inside this grocery store. When I came to the end of this isle, He pointed to you and said, "That's him! He's my Son, and I'm very proud of him!" Now I'm really asking myself, *"Seriously, where are the cameras?"* She just stood there with this huge grin on her face, and then said very directly, "You're very serious! You mean business!" "What did you just say?" I asked in shock. Again, it dawned on me that no one, with the exception of the cashier up front, was in the store. I mean, no one!

With an intent expression on her face and with great resolve in her voice, she said, "I need to pray for you. Can I put my hand on your heart?" What was I gonna say? "Yes," I answered, as she moved toward me, laid her small hand over my heart, closed her eyes and softly prayed, "Fire...Fire!, Jesus!"

With her hand still on my heart, she looked up at me and said, "When you open your mouth, you will speak with boldness, and with fire and you will prophesy and reach many people for the Lord." I was stunned, as I thanked and hugged her. No sooner had I done so, then she said, "I have to leave!" I need to pray for someone on the streets in Hollywood right now!" She smiled, turned, and quickly walked back down the aisle from where she came. When she got to the end and rounded the corner, something inside me told me to follow her. I hastily pushed my grocery cart to the end of the aisle, only to find out that she was nowhere to be found. She had totally vanished!

I immediately scanned the store, left the cart, and walked to a large window facing the parking lot to see if she was getting into a car. I saw nothing. Just a few cars, including my own. I stood there for a minute, looking out that window for any sign of movement. Again, nothing! I walked back to my cart and wheeled it to the one and only check stand that was open. I asked the cashier if he noticed a girl running out of the store just then? Without ever answering my question, he asked, "Would you like a bag?" as though he didn't hear me. "No thanks," I said, and proceeded to the nearest door. "Hang on a second", he said. "I need to unlock that door for you, so you can get out." I got chills as he walked to the front door with the store keys.

That night, I sat in my car for the longest time in a near empty parking lot, replaying in my mind, over and over again, exactly what had just transpired. I still have my questions, but one thing is crystal clear; God will do whatever it takes to get our attention! Why would He choose to do something so elaborate for someone like me? I'm nobody! I don't deserve it! But then again, maybe that's my answer.

The Good, The Sad and the Ugly

I started intensely praying for my dad this morning. I've prayed for him a lot in the past, but this was different. It was more urgent. There was clear cut direction and purpose. Most mornings ever since my stroke, I have a general idea of what I need to pray about or who I should be praying for. To some degree, a lot of my prayer life has been planned out in advance, but as the morning unfolds, specific issues or people will come to mind as the Lord directs me. But this particular morning was out of the ordinary. There was a definite sense of urgency concerning my father's wellbeing.

As this went on morning after morning, the prayers became more intense until I found myself literally groaning for my dad. Something was wrong, but I just couldn't put my finger on it. My dad was getting older, and it was becoming obvious to us all.

I remember feeling so sad for him as I prayed on his behalf. He had been alive for over eighty years without ever knowing true peace. To go through life all alone without Jesus broke my heart. It's a humbling experience when God puts it on our hearts to pray for one of His children, but you lose all objectivity when that child is your own father.

After a while, I found myself begging God to do "whatever it would take" to save my dad. The last honest conversation I had with him concerning God was shortly after I left the hospital in Vegas. We were on his back patio one evening, just him and I, and I asked him outright, "Dad, after all that's happened to me recently, do you have any new perspective on God?" My Dad thought for a second, stared straight ahead, and finally answered, "Don't get me wrong, Dave. Nothing against what you've gone through, but I still believe that when you die, there's nothing. No afterlife, just nothingness." That statement rang in my ears every morning after that. The thought of him being separated from God for the rest of eternity was too overwhelming for me to comprehend, and it became increasingly painful with each passing day.

Shortly after that conversation, I received a call from my mom. She was concerned. My Dad had been hearing voices which seemed to be emanating from the walls and throughout the house. They were whispering to each other when he would walk down the hallway or enter a bedroom. He would only hear them talking when my mother wasn't around. From the moment I was made aware of it, I suspected demonic activity. I just assumed God was pulling out all the stops, allowing it to happen as a means of inducing fear which would eventually bring him to Jesus. Nonetheless, it still concerned me, so I continued to pray for his salvation. I called my Dad to get the details. When he got on the phone, I could tell he was shaken. He told me about the voices, to which I replied, "are you talking back to them?" "Not yet," he chuckled.

I wanted to pray for him right there over the phone, but I knew he would think that would be inappropriate, so I refrained. Looking back, I wish I had. I wish I had told him how much I loved him, and even more importantly, how much God loved him.

The doctors explained away the episodes as being an improper dosage of blood-pressure medication, but I've come to realize that there is a spiritual significance to many things that we otherwise discount.

As I had mentioned, my Dad had been showing signs of aging over the past few months. He used to brag to all of us that every time he'd visit the doctor, he would walk out with a "clean bill of health." He had bypass surgery years ago, as well as small stroke two years earlier, but came out of them both with flying colors.

I knew something spiritually significant was happening to my dad. I also knew that faith in God was a battle between hope, and fear and from my perspective at the time, fear seemed to be winning out.

As I continued to push through in prayer each day, it started taking a toll, on both me, and my family. I was on edge all the time. I would snap at everyone around me, especially my wife. I was experiencing PTSD as well as seizures at a greater frequency.

The deeper I went in prayer and the greater the urgency for my dad's salvation, the more vulnerable I became to spiritual attack. What we do in prayer is no secret. Imagine wearing a red jumpsuit in a sea of white t-shirts. That's how easily the enemy can spot us when we pray. We can't see them, but rest assured they can see every move we make, and their goal isn't merely to slow us down or to sidetrack us, but to utterly destroy us and any resolve we may have in the future of entering into prayer again.

The spiritual forces that we battle against are that serious. They play for keeps, and they will do whatever it takes to thwart God's plan from being accomplished through our lives. Thank the Lord, I was able to eventually identify the attack and continue to push forward in prayer for my dad, realizing that it would probably get worse before it got better. I couldn't control what was going on around me, but one thing I could control was how I reacted to it. So again, I just kept praying, apologizing to my family and repenting of my sins.

One night, something really strange happened. Strange even for me. It was late, and my wife and kids had already gone to bed. I felt a strong desire to stay up and continue in prayer; so I did.

My dog Pepper, a small black lab, usually stays downstairs whenever I stay up late to keep me company. She has a bed next to the couch where I like to pray. I think she enjoys laying by the fireplace and keeping an eye on me, most likely in the hopes of getting a midnight snack.

At bedtime, Pepper has a ritual of checking every room before she finally settles down in our master bedroom. She was never a great guard dog, but always a good watchdog. She forces herself to stay awake until every last family member is home, in bed, and in their rightful place. While I think it messes with her routine when I stay up late at times, somehow I think she knew something was wrong that night. Pepper has been part of our family for fifteen years. She's the only dog my children have ever known, faithfully standing by their sides from preschool to college. She's a sensitive dog. Sometimes she seems to bark at nothing. My wife says it's because she's old, half-blind and deaf, but I like to think its because she's seeing things in the spirit realm and even talking to angels. Many times when I pray, I'll look over and see her watching me very intensely, almost like she's keenly aware of what's happening in the moment. She might not always comprehend what's going on, but she definitely knows when we're hurting. That night, I was hurting beyond belief.

As I began to pray, something came over me. I pleaded with God give me more time with my Dad. If he was around just a little longer, then maybe he would come to know Jesus; or at least that was my desire. I continued with that one request for quite some time. I almost felt like I was chasing God to get His attention. I had deep concerns that He wasn't listening to me. At one point, I began begging Him to reveal Himself to my dad. I cried, and begged, and begged some more. I continued doing so until I was exhausted.

It was about 2:00 am before I realized that I needed sleep. I decided tomorrow would be another day. I motioned to my dog to follow me upstairs, watching her sniff every door as I turned off the lights. The minute my head hit the pillow, I was out, and so was Pepper. I fell into a deep sleep for about an hour and a half before I was woken up at exactly 3:30 am. I remember the time because my alarm clock had big red numbers which seemed to be blaring in my face at the time. To my left, I noticed a dark silhouette next to my bed, just staring at me. As my eyes focused, sure enough, it was my dog. "What are you doing, Pepper?" I said, as she stood there looking intently at me. "Go lay down! right now!" I said in my authoritative voice. She didn't move, as I proceeded to snap my fingers and point to her bed which was positioned at the foot of mine. As Pepper reluctantly walked back to her bed, I fell back to sleep. Five minutes later, I rolled to the edge of my bed, and once again, opened my eyes to that same dark silhouette; this time, right in front of my face. I spoke sternly to her again, just to have her walk over to our closed bedroom door and swipe at it with her paw. This is usually her way of saying, "I'm thirsty!" or "I have to pee!" Feeling for my dog, I decided to indulge her.

When we got downstairs, I proceeded to open the kitchen door to our backyard. Pepper didn't go outside like she would usually do if she needed to do her business. Instead, she just stared at me, so I closed the door and filled up her water bowl. Again, she just stared at me as she walked over to the same couch where I often pray, and laid down on her bed which was sitting right in front of it. Her eyes followed me as I walked over to her. "What do you want?" I asked. She just looked up at me with those big eyes as I sat down next to her.

Immediately, my mind went to my Dad. Instantly, God's Spirit flooded the room, as I once again was drawn into intense prayer. This continued for about two hours, and then, as quickly as it began, it was over. I looked back at my dog, and said, "Are you ready to go back to bed?"

Pepper is one hundred and five in dog years, so getting up and around is not the same for her as it used to be. We both made our way up the long staircase and back to bed just as the sun was coming up. I fell into a deep sleep, until I was suddenly interrupted by the sound of the garage door opening.

It was somewhere around 8:30 am. My wife had already gone to work. She worked only one block away, so I was used to hearing the occasional noise of the garage door whenever she'd come home for whatever reason. Seconds later, I heard the door leading into the house open, as someone bypassed the kitchen and began making their way upstairs. I could tell by the familiar pace of her steps that it was my wife. I immediately pulled the sheets and comforter over my head and began pleading with God. I already knew why she had come home that morning.

In a desperate attempt to change the outcome, my pleading became louder, until I felt a hand touch my shoulder. It was Robynn. She sat on the edge of our bed in silence. For some reason, I thought if I just hid under the covers, the truth of what she was about to tell me would just go away. It didn't. Like a child in trouble, I slowly pulled the sheets down to the bridge of my nose and looked into my wife's sad eyes. "Your brother just called me," she hesitated. "Your Dad is gone."

The Story that never ends!

One would think that every story has an ending. With every good book, television show or movie, there's always a beginning, a middle and an end. That's the way it's always been, and that's the way we like it. Predictable! We enjoy seeing every trial and situation in life–wrapped up, in a pretty little package, ready to be presented to us with a nice big bow on top! Well, with God, it doesn't always work that way. That's a concept that Hollywood invented and we have all grown accustomed to. If that were true, my dad would still be alive, my prayers would have all been answered, and he would have finally found Jesus and lived out his remaining days with his family, knowing and loving God. Unfortunately, that's not at all what happened.

Immediately after my Dad's death, I flew to Seattle where my parents lived, to help prepare for the funeral. I was a mess. I was furious with God for what He had done to me. I trusted Him. I asked Him to heal my Dad and to extend his life so that he might finally be saved. I just wanted my dad to go to heaven. That was it! When I asked God to do "Whatever it takes," I didn't mean He should kill him! I was in torment. My inner struggle to understand why this happened took a toll on my family. Instead of being a source of comfort for my Mother, I was a time bomb ready to explode, and I eventually did! The first morning, after arriving in Seattle, my brother and his wife were in our parent's kitchen, helping with the arrangements for the memorial service. Out of nowhere, I snapped! Let's just say, my attitude at the time was less than exemplary.

I was mad at God, and it was evident in the way I was treating others. Something rooted deep in my heart had to be addressed, and that was my extreme anger with God.

All the love Jesus showed me in the hospital and all the peace and joy that followed me around day after day, just disappeared! It was like a hurricane came in and whisked it all away! I quickly realized that I was of no use to anyone around me, and wallowing in my own pity party, I decided to find a hotel room and go sleep till the next morning. *"Maybe that would help me regain my composure,"* I rationalized. Well, that one night turned into a total of three days and two nights.

That first day, I did nothing but pace the floor of my hotel room and pray. To be honest, I wouldn't call it praying. It was more like whining. I knew I couldn't change a thing. What was done was done, but that didn't mean I had to accept it. So I continued to pace, scream into my pillow, and try to understand God's logic. It was pathetic! I acted like a four year old being denied candy.

On the third morning, I received a call from my good friend Earl Blevins. Earl is a former pro rodeo cowboy and bareback rider, who is now a professional rodeo judge. He's also a seminary student, a man of prayer, and one of my "go to guys" when I need spiritual clarity. Out of the blue, Earl called just to see how I was feeling, He heard about my dad passing away, and was just keeping tabs on me like he always has. Earl has known our family for well over thirty years, and is loved and respected by all of us; especially my dad. When I answered the phone, Earl could tell that I was in a bad way. I couldn't fake it with him. He knew me too well. I was drowning in the circumstances of what had happened, and needed someone to throw me a rope. So he did! Earl simply said, "You know the faith you have in Jesus for your own salvation?" I grunted out a "yes." "Then use that same faith and hope for your dad," he said in his familiar Oklahoma accent. That was it! After that, he prayed for me and said good-bye.

I immediately got on my knees and began to repent. I was ashamed of how I treated God. He didn't deserve that from me! I realized at that moment that God had not moved away from me one inch. I was the one who had moved away from Him. He loved my dad and always wanted the best for him! He also honored my prayers of concern for him. I know that now, although I didn't see it then. While I was in the midst of repentance, I had a vision in my mind. Through it, God was once again reinforcing the fact that He was in complete control of everything!

I saw my Dad sitting up in his bed and reaching out for Jesus's hand. He was being offered a place in His

Kingdom. My Mother told me later that she found him in his bed, lying on his back, arms neatly folded and with a peaceful expression on his face.

'Thank you Jesus!'

I get embarrassed when I look back at how I behaved during that chapter of my life. And ashamed! Ashamed of how I treated my family, and especially how I treated God.

All the while, I assumed my dad's story had ended. I initially assumed that he was taken from us and that was it. He was separated from God and separated from his family forever, and I immediately blamed Jesus! Little did I know, my dad's story hadn't ended at all. In fact, it was just beginning.

JAMES NEILL FRIDLUND
1937–2017

"We'll miss you Dad, till we see you again!"

Final Thoughts

In the end, it's not about battling demons, seeing angels or sneaking a glimpse of eternity. It's about loving Jesus, and knowing that He is in control of it all.

When Jesus rose from the dead, He visited the disciples, but Thomas, one of the twelve, was not with the others when He appeared to them. "We have seen the Lord," they all said. But, Thomas said to them, "Unless I see in His hands the marks of the nails, and put my finger into the nail holes, and put my hand into His side, I will never believe."

Eight days later, the disciples were together again, and this time Thomas was with them. Just then, Jesus walked right through the barred door of the house they were gathered in and stood among them and said, "Peace be with you." Then He said to Thomas, "Reach here with your finger, and see My hands; and put out your hand and place it in my side. Do not be unbelieving, but believe!" Thomas answered Him, "My Lord and my God." Jesus then said to him, "Because you have seen me, do you now believe?"

I imagine, at that moment, that Thomas was speechless.

Jesus went on to say, "Thomas, because you have seen me, you now believe, but blessed are those who have not seen and still believe."

The book of John goes on to say, *"Many other signs and wonders were performed by Jesus that day, in the presence of His disciples, which are not written in this book."*

To this day, those signs and wonders are a mystery.

What was written and passed down through generations, was done so for one simple reason; **that** *we might believe Jesus is the Christ, the Son of the living God; and through believing, we might have life through His name. (John 20:24-31)*

We must always remember that we will never fully understand the mysteries of His Kingdom, and only when we see Him face to face will our understanding be expanded.

Since the fall of Adam, man's relationship with God has been greatly hindered and limited. Only The Father can decide when and to whom those secrets will be revealed. Until then, we need to love and believe in His Son, and to know that *His grace is sufficient for us. (2 Corinthians 12:9)*

For now, we see through a dark glass; but then face to face; now I know in part; but then I shall know fully, even as I am fully known. (1 Corinthians 13:12)

No longer will there be any curse. The throne of God and of the Lamb will be in the city, and His servants will serve Him. They will see His face, and His name will be on their foreheads. There will be no more night. They will not need the light of a lamp or the light of the sun, for the Lord God will give them light, and they will reign forever and ever. (Revelation 22:3-5)

Dear reader,

I want to thank you for taking the time to read my story.

If you're hurting for any reason, Jesus wants to take your burdens. That's what He does, and that's why He is alive today! Drop your guard and let Him in. He'll never hurt you, He'll never disappoint you, and He will never, ever leave you!

"When you pass through the waters, I will be with you." (Isaiah 43:2)

"But these three remain; FAITH, HOPE, and LOVE...and the greatest of these is LOVE" (1st Corinthians 13:12)

Always know, Jesus loves you because HE IS LOVE!

He does not care about what you've done. All He cares about is you!

Pray right now. Jesus will meet you right where you are. You can be real with Him. Just lay your secrets down and repent. (Acts 17:30)

He's faithful and just to forgive them...all of them! (1 John 1:19)

If there's a take away from my story, It would simply be that Jesus begins where you end.

Dave

OUTTAKES

The following is an ongoing collection of random posts highlighting the goodness of God through my eyes, as He continues to do what He does best; mold my life for His glory!

POST #42- March 29, 2017

I've been in and out of the hospital three times in the last three years! Each time I would leave to go home, I would leave a different person. A person of greater humility; humbled by God's grace and goodness. With each incident, the Lord broke me a little more, so He could put me back together exactly the way that He desires.

I've finally come to the understanding that the only way to be more like Jesus is to become completely broken, stripped of all pride and conceit, having absolutely no hope in life apart from Him! Transformation is a process. It doesn't happen overnight. Sometimes it's a long and grueling process, but it's a process nonetheless.

We, as American Christians, are too preoccupied with results. We have become a results oriented society. When we get sick, we want to be healed instantaneously. When we go through financial hardship, we expect an immediate "financial breakthrough." When we're down, we expect to immediately get back up. We want, we want, we want!

Don't get me wrong; I'm still results oriented. I've just decided the final result I want is a deeper relationship with Jesus, no matter the cost! *(Luke:14:27-33)*

Two weeks before my trip to Las Vegas with my wife Robynn, I'd been having a hard time. I was falling back into my old ways. My attitude was horrible, I was constantly worried about everything, and was very insensitive to members of my family and those around me.

I had completely lost the peace and joy that Jesus had so graciously given me just months earlier, and managed to replace it with the cares of this world. The sad part was that everything was going great! We were thriving! I loved my job, we had plenty of money, everyone in my family was healthy; we were living the dream! There was just one problem. I was slowly dying inside. Each day that passed, it seemed like I was getting further and further away from the Lord, until one night I found myself sitting in a hotel room in Huntsville, Alabama at three o'clock in the morning, begging Jesus to do "whatever it would take to bring me back into His presence." I had a taste of His presence, and when you see a glimpse of that reality, nothing else could ever satisfy. I was like a drug addict, and my drug of choice was the Spirit of God!. I wasn't sure how to get it back though. Do I read the Bible more? Do I try really hard to be a better person, to be more like Jesus? All I knew was that I felt completely separated from Him, and I was willing to do whatever it took in order to feel His presence again in my life.

Two weeks later, I was in the ICU at Sunrise Hospital in Las Vegas, and the rest of the story is history. That's what it took!

POST #43–May 17, 2017

The Lord's good!

Wow! I'm sitting in a hotel room in Washington DC, minding my own business, when all of a sudden the Lord just showed up "Big Time!" I had not felt His presence like that in a while. I had panic attacks at work all day, and came back to my hotel room totally defeated. As I laid down on my bed and closed my eyes to pray, Jesus literally flooded the room with His presence. I don't even know how to describe it. I just know that when we are weak and empty, He is there to fill us up!

It's indescribable. I don't know how to explain it other than that I'm just so appreciative for my life, my family, my friends, and the fact that I can share my experiences with all of you without judgement. Jesus is real, and I want everyone to feel what I'm feeling right now. He just loves us so much! If He can love me, He can love anyone!

POST #44- September 17, 2017

The Mirror Image

I'm coming up on almost one year since my stroke. I've had a lot of time to ponder about the amazing things that God has done for me this past year. Never before have I tried, or even cared to please God like I have these past months. I've been going over and over in my mind why it is that I've been experiencing so many blessings in so many areas of my life. I've also tried to pinpoint the difference in me now as opposed to the Dave that walked this planet just a year ago. Through a series of recent events, I think the Lord has shown me the answer. I was reading the Bible this evening, and came across this Scripture:

"But be doers of the word, and not hearers only, deceiving yourselves.

For if anyone is a hearer of the word and not a doer, he is like a man who looks intently at his natural face in a mirror. For he looks at himself and goes away....and immediately forgets what he was like. But the one who looks into the perfect law, the law of liberty, and perseveres, being no longer a hearer who forgets, but a doer who acts, he will be blessed in his doing."

James 1:22-25

Jesus has radically, permanently changed me forever. But part of that change will always be to never forget what the old me was like.

POST #45–September 18, 2017

Yes, God has blessed me beyond measure this past year!!

Here's the short list, and I'm compelled to share it as an expression of my gratitude:

1. Knowing Jesus has my back no matter what!
2. Waking up in the middle of the night and seeing my wife sleeping next to me!
3. Having my daughters text me for no other reason than just to tell me they love me!
4. Getting a call from my oldest Son who's away at college, and staying up till all hours of the night talking about how awesome Jesus is!
5. Being asked by my second Son to speak at his High School FCA group (Fellowship of Christian Athletes), where he is a leader!
6. Having my youngest Son wait for me in the living room, so we can watch, and even pray for the Seahawks game after church!
7. Being able to spend time with my beautiful grandchildren, and knowing I'll get to see them grow up!

8. Having my family and friends call me to pray for them!

YES, this is the short list!

My life in no way is perfect, but the greatest blessing in it is the knowledge that
IT IS NOT, and NEVER AGAIN WILL BE my life!

POST #46–February 8, 2018

I JUST WANT TO BE WITH YOU!

When I was in the hospital, on life support and sitting with Jesus, all I cared about was being with Him. I remember thinking momentarily about my wife and kids, and how I'd miss them if I ended up going to Heaven. No sooner had that thought entered my mind before I immediately blurted out, "I love my wife and kids Lord, but I don't want to be with them, I just want to be with you!"

When I look back at that moment, I remember the fear and desperation I felt, thinking I might be separated from Him; even for a minute!

Only recently, have I come to understand the following Scripture:

Matthew 10:34
"Do not suppose that I have come to bring peace to the earth. I did not come to bring peace, but a sword. For I have come to turn a man against his father, a daughter against her mother, a daughter-in-law

against her mother-in-law - a man's enemies will be the members of his own household. Anyone who loves their father or mother more than me is not worthy of me; anyone who loves their son or daughter more than me is not worthy of me. Whoever does not take up their cross and follow me is not worthy of me."

Jesus